CONQUEST

*Pete Carroll and the Trojans'
Climb to the Top of the
College Football Mountain*

David Wharton and Gary Klein

*To a pair
of USC fans
from way back
D Wht*

*Jim & Bernice,
Hope you enjoy the
book and many
more Conquests!*

TRIUMPH
B O O K S
CHICAGO

Library of Congress Cataloging-in-Publication Data

Wharton, David, 1961–
    Conquest : Pete Carroll and the Trojans' climb to the top of the college football mountain / David Wharton and Gary Klein.
        p. cm.
    Includes index.
    ISBN-13: 978-1-57243-789-0
    ISBN-10: 1-57243-789-8
    1. University of Southern California—Football. 2. Southern California Trojans (Football team). 3. Carroll, Pete, 1951–   I. Klein, Gary, 1960–
II. Title.

GV958.U5857W43 2005
796.332'63'0979494—dc22

2005048506

This book is available in quantity at special discounts for your group or organization. For further information, contact:

Triumph Books
    542 South Dearborn Street
    Suite 750
    Chicago, Illinois 60605
    (312) 939-3330
    Fax (312) 663-3557

Printed in U.S.A.
ISBN-13: 978-1-57243-789-0
ISBN-10: 1-57243-789-8
Design and page production by Patricia Frey; editorial production by Prologue Publishing Services, LLC.
Photos copyright © 2002–2003 by the *Los Angeles Times* unless indicated otherwise. Reprinted with permission.

For Mo and Zack.
—D.W.

For Kathy, Casey, Chris, Will, and Matt. The best team ever.
—G.K.

Contents

Foreword

From the 61st row of the Coliseum, I could barely see the USC Trojans run onto the field, but it did not matter. It was 1964, I was 11 years old, and my father was sitting next to me. Father and son enjoying football together, it happens every autumn. My father loved sports, but he had no connection with USC; he was a Flying Dutchman of Hofstra University in New York. But for me, that very first game was the beginning of a 40-year relationship with USC and its football program.

Over the years, I sat in those uncomfortable seats and watched the likes of Mike Garrett as he defied the gods and popped out of the other side of a scrum of would-be tacklers; I was stunned by the last-minute heroics of Craig Fertig and Rod Sherman as they denied Notre Dame an undefeated season with an improbable touchdown; I was there when Gary Beban and O. J. Simpson battled for bragging rights in Los Angeles; I was the lucky participant on USC teams in the early seventies that never lost a game in the Coliseum, never lost a Pac-8 game, and won two national championships; I saw and played for John McKay and John Robinson when they coached and cajoled their teams to dozens of victories.

Yet, in my 40-plus years of watching USC football, no era has been better than the past few years under head coach Pete Carroll. What he has done in his brief four-year tenure is quite remarkable. This new era of Trojans football, so well captured by David Wharton and

Conquest

Gary Klein in *Conquest,* comes after a malaise in the storied program that had Trojans fans and network executives longing for a past that seemed impossible to resurrect. Many, myself included, felt that USC football had seen its best days and would not, could not, return to the days when John McKay coached and wisecracked his way to four national championships and eight Rose Bowl appearances.

Pete Carroll has not only resurrected a moribund program, he has made it fun again. His teams the past three years have not only been dominant (I never thought an opponent could score 55 points against an Oklahoma team that made it to the national championship game), but these teams have been more entertaining to watch than any team I have ever seen at USC or played on in the seventies. Whether you sit in row 61, on the 50-yard line, or at home in front of the TV, it cannot be denied that the Pete Carroll teams of the past three years have been stunningly good.

Conquest is an intriguing story about how a program was turned around and about how hard, yet rewarding, that can be. While only a game, the recent rise in the football fortunes of USC captured in this book reminds me of how invigorating a sport can be.

—Pat Haden

Acknowledgments

This book could not have been written without the help of a great many people. Thanks go to our editors at the *Los Angeles Times*, Bill Dwyre, Dave Morgan, and Mike Hiserman. Also to the kind and talented writers with whom we have worked, including Bill Plaschke, T. J. Simers, Chris Dufresne, Rob Fernas, Paul Gutierrez, Robyn Norwood, Lonnie White, Steve Henson, Richard Winton, Ben Bolch, Sam Farmer, and Mike DiGiovanna. Karen Chaderjian pored over each and every page, as did Hans Tesselaar and Jerry Crowe. Tim Tessalone and his USC sports information staff helped with questions. It should also be noted that anyone who writes about USC football owes a debt of gratitude to the late *Los Angeles Times* sportswriter Mal Florence. Most of all, thanks to our friends and families.

CHAPTER 1

A Defining Moment

It wasn't until midday that a storm blew into South Florida, a damp wind gathering in swirls, rattling through trees that lined the football field. Players looked up, checking the sky, and the next minute it was pouring, streaks of rain splashing off helmets and shoulder pads. The linemen put their heads down, kept sloshing, grunting through drills. The quarterback kept zipping passes to his receivers.

If anything, the conditions at USC practice that day—the last day of 2004—put a grin on Pete Carroll's face. As if it were the best thing that could have happened. From a purely football point of view, the coach wanted to see his guys deal with a little adversity, trying not to mishandle any snaps or fumble the ball. For entirely different reasons, it seemed like the kid in him got downright excited, sopping wet, gray curls matted against his forehead. Carroll splashed through puddles. He laughed.

"This is great," he called out to no one in particular. And later: "Man, I wish I could put on some pads."

His attitude was infectious, the team growing more boisterous as the afternoon wore on. Anyone who had been around the Trojans knew their practices moved at a rapid clip—nobody, but nobody, ever walked. When the horn sounded, players hustled to the next spot, led by assistants barking, moving even faster. Scrimmages were conducted at full speed. "We're all jumping around," said Reggie

Bush, the young tailback. "You would think we're playing a real game." No Florida squall could slow them.

Afterward, in a makeshift locker room, soaked jerseys strewn across an indoor basketball court, the mood remained upbeat as players chatted with family. Shaun Cody, the All-American defensive lineman, shrugged off the weather, saying, "We can play in whatever the conditions." Like buddies having fun in the rain. No hint of worry or nerves, nothing to suggest that he and his teammates were facing the biggest game of their lives.

In four more days, the Trojans would play Oklahoma in the FedEx Orange Bowl to decide the national championship of college football. A meeting of undefeated teams. No. 1 versus No. 2. Fans had waited for this game since summer, watching as the squads dominated tough opponents and, on lesser days, found ways to get by. There had been some squabbling over the bowl championship series, or BCS, the complicated formula that determined the title game. Another undefeated team, Auburn, had been left out of the mix, but it was hard to argue this matchup. Two schools rich in football tradition. Two teams that had led the polls from wire to wire. Never before had there been so much star power on one field.

Start with Matt Leinart, the USC quarterback. He was a remarkable story, a once-pudgy kid who needed surgery to fix his crossed eyes and took up football only at his older brother's urging. Now he was the best player in the land, winner of the Heisman Trophy. The Trojans also had Bush, whose humble nature belied a showman's flair, a propensity for cutback runs and dazzling kick returns. "He has such an ability to create yards, to make you miss, and to make big plays," said Bob Stoops, the Oklahoma coach. The Sooners answered with quarterback Jason White, the Heisman winner from the year before, coming back for one more try at the championship that had eluded him. This time, he had help in the form of Adrian Peterson, a freshman sensation at running back, the sort of talent that came along once in a generation. Both defenses were tough and opportunistic. Both lineups were studded with All-Americans.

"So many great athletes," Bush said. "It could play out to be an instant classic."

The media were already using terms such as "historic" and "best ever" to describe the upcoming game at Pro Player Stadium. If any more hype were necessary, it was provided by a young defensive lineman for the Sooners. Shortly before the teams arrived in Florida, Larry Birdine told reporters that Leinart was "definitely overrated . . . he's a good quarterback but not a Heisman-winning quarterback." The big sophomore, known for uttering whatever crossed his mind, did not stop there. He spoke of watching the Trojans on film and deciding, "They're an average team." It was a startling bit of trash talk given that both squads were stocked with veterans who otherwise knew to keep their mouths shut. The USC players brushed it off. "Just a guy talking," Leinart said. "I just kind of laughed." Yet, in an unintended way, Birdine's comments had touched a nerve.

Carroll acknowledged as much on that rainy day after practice. Long after everyone else had gone inside, he stayed on the field to play catch with someone's son, a boy who had come out to watch. He waved a hand and told the kid to go deep, lofted an easy spiral that was caught in clumsy arms. Carroll let out a whoop. Despite the loose atmosphere, everyone having a good time, the coach said, "This is huge for us."

It was much more than one game, one season. The Trojans needed to prove themselves in a bigger way.

———

Heritage Hall stands near the center of the University of Southern California campus, a seventies building of traditional red brick set against more flamboyant architectural elements—high arches and slender columns. In the lobby, with its plush red carpeting, display cases hold artifacts of the school's football past, the national championship trophies and six bronze Heismans. Beyond that is a staircase leading to a cluster of offices on the second floor. It was up there, shortly after the regular season ended, that preparations for the Orange Bowl began.

Much of the work was done in a corner office, coaches gathering each day around a conference table. With the lights dimmed, they watched hours of game film on a big screen, pausing, reversing, poring over each detail of Oklahoma's season. In some ways, they were looking in a mirror, the teams remarkably alike, right down to the All-American defensive lineman named Cody—USC's Shaun and Oklahoma's Dan—that each had on the roster. "Our numbers are so comparable in points allowed and all of those areas," Carroll said. "There's just a ton of similarities."

The more film the USC coaches watched, the more they focused on Oklahoma's offensive line, built around Outland Trophy–winner Jammal Brown at right tackle. Most experts figured the Sooners held the advantage in this area. As Shaun Cody said, "They're going to try to pound us." Yet, in private, defensive line coach Ed Orgeron wasn't impressed by the left side of the line and suspected that his stout defensive tackle, Mike Patterson, could raise havoc in the middle. Of course, there was still the matter of tackling that young Sooners running back. "He's not the type of guy you just hit and he'll fall down," Patterson said. "You have to wrap him up . . . we have to swarm him."

The other detail that stood out on film was Oklahoma's secondary. Twice, in close victories over Oklahoma State and Texas A&M, the Sooners had given up a slew of long passes. Granted, they were playing without senior Antonio Perkins, who had since returned from injury. And their defense had improved further when freshman cornerback Marcus Walker joined the starting lineup in November. Still, the Trojans' figured to test them deep.

A Defining Moment

Even after the game plan was finished and given to the team in a series of practices, the USC coaches kept going back to the film room—"The deeper the study, the more you see," Carroll said—looking for tidbits, jotting more notes until the day the Trojans headed east. They touched down in South Florida shortly after dark on December 28, stepping off the plane to a fanfare of music and dancers, potted palms and an orange carpet rolled out on the tarmac. Buses emblazoned with giant photographs of Carroll and former USC quarterback Carson Palmer waited to take them to their beachfront hotel.

Many of the players remembered the Westin Diplomat from a previous stay, when the Trojans faced Iowa in the 2003 Orange Bowl. They knew about the gleaming lobby and art deco architecture, the palatial grounds with a mirrored pool that emptied in matching waterfalls to a lagoon below. Seniors got private rooms, a luxury that came around only once a year, though Cody wasn't so sure he liked the idea. Down the hall, his younger teammates hollered and laughed. "I'm going to be kind of bored," he said. "I'll probably just go and hang out at somebody else's room."

The Trojans began daily practices the next afternoon at a small college campus north of Miami, the coaches realistic about how much could be accomplished. They knew that a good part of the week would be spent dealing with distractions, including a handful of celebrities that hovered around the team. Nick Lachey, the MTV star, was a Leinart pal, and comedian Will Ferrell was a big fan. Tommy Lasorda, former manager of the Los Angeles Dodgers, stopped by. So did USC legend Frank Gifford, who quipped, "Just don't tell them the year I played . . . I don't think their fathers were born." There were Orange Bowl events to attend—dinners, parties, hospital visits—as well as the lure of clubs along South Beach.

Back in 2003, Leinart had taken full advantage. He was a third-stringer then, "hanging out" and doing "all the fun things." This time, he said, would be different.

Conquest

———

The Sooners had arrived in South Florida a day earlier than USC and had gone straight from the airport to another college near the ocean—their training site for the week—where they ran drills until sunset. "Our schedule is crazy," one of the players said, coming off the field. "Straight off the plane we rushed here."

They were back at it the next afternoon, working out behind locked gates, a uniformed security guard standing post. By the time USC arrived that evening, Oklahoma had finished its second full session, including a 35-play scrimmage. The mood was different from practices back home, said Peterson, the running back, "more aggressive . . . getting into the right mind-set for a big game." Or, as quarterback Jason White explained, "We're down here for one reason."

They had a score to settle.

Oklahoma had won the 2000 national championship at the Orange Bowl and looked for all the world like a dynasty in the making when it returned to the BCS title game—this time at the Nokia Sugar Bowl—only three years later. But at that point, the Sooners' storybook tale took a wrong turn. Facing underdog Louisiana State, they started slowly and fell short with a fourth-quarter rally, losing by a touchdown. "We learned our lesson," said Brown, the offensive tackle. "You can't just roll into the championship game and expect to win."

Attitude wasn't the only problem. That squad struggled to run the ball, putting too big a burden on the quarterback. So Stoops and his assistants devoted their off-season to going after Peterson, the best schoolboy back in the country. They stole him away from neighboring Texas and, by the third game of the season, he was running wild. More than 200 yards against Oklahoma State. Three touchdowns against Baylor. Three more in the Big 12 championship versus

Colorado. The quiet freshman had two things going for him. First, he was tireless—hence the nickname "AD," as in "all day." Second, he ran with a bruising, straight-ahead style that forced defenses to make a choice.

"They have to decide whether they're going to try to stop the run or the pass," White said. "It's kind of like, pick your poison."

The Oklahoma players swore they were a different team with Peterson in the backfield. They had a 12–0 record in the regular season to back that claim, but now came time to prove it on a bigger stage. Thus the closed practices and decidedly serious atmosphere. An athletic department spokesman let it be known, from the very first day, that the talkative Birdine was off-limits. Reporters wondered if Stoops might reconsider.

"You want to talk to him today? You can talk to him," the coach said. Then, after a moment's pause, "Well, maybe you can't."

If Carroll was animated and energetic, Stoops was midwestern tough, the son of a high school coach who had grown up amid the steel mills of Youngstown, Ohio. His no-nonsense demeanor fit perfectly in Norman, a town on the Oklahoma plains where the university dominated the landscape and football was tantamount to religion. Stoops knew how much this Orange Bowl meant to the fans. Only a few weeks earlier, after the conference championship, his team had arrived home to "thousands of people at 3:00 or 4:00 in the morning," he said. "I like the fact that we're expected to win every week."

He also seemed to welcome questions about the previous season's disappointment against LSU, as if he wanted his guys to remember the hurt, to carry a chip on their shoulders. Back in training camp, they had adopted "Finish" as their rallying cry and had worn this motto on T-shirts and bracelets all season long. White had decided to stick around for his final season, in large part, to get another shot at the title. A victory over USC would put Oklahoma back on top of the college game, with two championships in five years. It would make everything right again.

"They want to finish," Stoops said of his players. "They want to rectify what happened."

———

The big game was still five days away, the experts still debating over who might win, calling it a toss-up, when an event on the other side of the country changed everything.

Texas Tech defeated California, 45–31, in the Pacific Life Holiday Bowl at San Diego. This was the same Texas Tech that had lost decisively to Oklahoma earlier in the season. The same Cal that had come so close to upsetting USC, missing on four chances from point-blank range in the last two minutes. Now came the hue and cry. The Pacific-10 Conference was clearly overrated. USC had built its 12–0 record against inferior opponents.

One after another, sportswriters and television commentators began picking Oklahoma. The Sooners were too tough and too experienced, they reasoned, and Peterson would be unstoppable. The USC players claimed not to care about any predictions. "You can throw all that stuff out the window," safety Jason Leach said. Yet, as the Orange Bowl drew closer, there was another, more tangible reason for questioning their chances.

His name was LenDale White.

While Reggie Bush grabbed most of the spotlight, always showing up on highlight films, White was the other half of USC's tailback combo. He was a more powerful runner, an every-down back who could pound out three yards here, four yards there. He also served as a leader for the team, more outwardly emotional than Bush, thumping his chest, getting guys fired up in the huddle. All season long, the Trojans had alternated their so-called "Thunder and Lightning" sophomores, keeping defenses off-balance with two very different running styles. But White had sprained an ankle against UCLA and now, in Florida, was walking with a limp. Norm Chow, the offensive coordinator, said the team was prepared to go without him in the lineup. "You just have to make adjustments and keep rolling along," he said. "We just have to keep going."

The truth was, USC needed White. Offensive lineman John Drake explained, "If our offense was a courtroom, LenDale White would be the gavel."

Each day brought a new development. White was held out of practice or he ran a few drills but did not take part in scrimmages. The young man grew increasingly anxious. "I'll do anything I can to play," he said. "If I have to suck up the pain for two hours, three hours, that's what I'm going to do." He begged for more work, only to have his coach refuse. He said, "I'm going to get in [Carroll's] ear and let him know I'm ready to go." Finally, Carroll's wife got involved.

It was several days before kickoff, and a group of USC players were standing around the hotel. According to White, Glena Carroll approached and asked about his ankle. She then held her hands in the vicinity of the injury and said a short prayer. It might have seemed crazy, but "the next morning I woke up and it felt great," White said. The day after that, Carroll announced the tailback had his best practice in almost a month.

What were the chances? A big game—if not an entire season—saved by a spontaneous blessing? White wondered aloud if Glena might be his guardian angel. When *Los Angeles Times* columnist Bill Plaschke asked Pete Carroll about his wife's reputed curative powers, the coach could only grin and say, "All I know is, I'm very rarely sick."

Conquest

———

Great masses of clouds rumbled off in the distance—the rains that had soaked South Florida for several days were finally moving on. Carroll stepped outside the team hotel and found an empty veranda overlooking the ocean, a place to sit in the sun for a few minutes. He wore shorts and sandals, a dark pullover. Falling back on a chaise lounge, he began to talk about how badly he wanted to win this game.

"Nobody has beaten them this season," he said of the Sooners. "We'll have to overcome big odds."

There was something more—the weight of history hung over his team. For so long, USC football had known great success, with national championships dating to 1928, an aristocratic bloodline that ran from Cotton Warburton through Jon Arnett, from Mike Garrett through O. J. Simpson, from Charles White through Marcus Allen. But the eighties and nineties had brought hard times. The so-called "Tailback U." struggled to run the ball. There were unbearable losing streaks against rivals UCLA and Notre Dame. Trips to the Rose Bowl, once considered a birthright, had grown increasingly rare.

Fans began to wonder when the dry spell would end. Critics suggested that USC might never recapture its glory days.

Carroll's arrival in 2001 had not done much to raise hopes. Twice fired by the NFL, he was not USC's first choice and, by his own admission, had reached a difficult point in his career. "It was really clear that if I had another chance to be head coach, it was going to be my last chance," he said. "I had to get my act in order." Fans and alumni howled in protest. The new guy had not coached in college for more than a decade and, besides, he had some curious ideas about rebuilding the program, talking about defense in a conference known for passing the ball. Even worse, he had a reputation as a player's coach, friendly, certainly not the type to whip an ailing legacy back into shape.

Yet, after a rocky first year, Carroll had started his team on an astounding run. The Trojans finished the 2002 season with only two losses, crushing Iowa in that Orange Bowl. In 2003, with only one loss, they were kept out of the championship game by the controversial BCS formula but earned a share of the title by dominating Michigan in the Rose Bowl. Now, in Carroll's fourth season, they were on the verge of something even better.

Gazing out over the Atlantic Ocean, the prospect of a historic victory on the horizon, Carroll said, "This is fun. Absolutely." In the weeks to come, he would face the potential break up of this team, his quarterback thinking of turning pro, Chow and other assistants considering jobs elsewhere, but for now all the pieces were in place. Reporters had mentioned that a win over Oklahoma—and back-to-back championships—might qualify USC as a modern dynasty. "The big 'D' word," Carroll had said with a laugh, quickly switching to another topic. But there was no avoiding the issue.

The Trojans were looking for a big finish. Something that would put them indisputably back on top of the college football world. Something every bit as amazing and unexpected as the past four seasons.

CHAPTER 2

Dark Days

To appreciate this tale of football rebirth, it is important to know what came before. Go back to the fall of 2000, the season before Pete Carroll arrived, the Trojans playing their opener against Penn State. They were leading and, midway through the third quarter, could see their opponent wearing out. So the offensive linemen made a simple request: "Let us run it down their throats."

Time and again, tailback Sultan McCullough charged into the line. A few yards here, a few yards there. Simple but effective.

His tough running not only sealed a 29–5 victory at Giants Stadium in East Rutherford, New Jersey, it took the pressure off quarterback Carson Palmer, who looked rusty after missing much of the previous season with an injury. The defense helped, too, standing its ground against a traditional East Coast powerhouse that was supposed to be bigger and stronger. Paul Hackett, the USC coach at the time, could not hide his delight. "I just loved the way we played . . . the enthusiasm, the excitement, the emotion," he said. "This was about a bunch of guys who wanted to be different from the last couple of years."

By then, the glory days at USC were but a memory. Two decades had passed since the last national championship—almost that long since the last Heisman Trophy winner—and too many seasons had ended with the team settling for an invitation to the Freedom Bowl or the John Hancock Bowl or no bowl at all. One after another, coaches came and went. Ted Tollner, Larry Smith, John Robinson. The school had hired Hackett in 1998, coaxing him away from the Kansas City Chiefs with a five-year, $3.5-million deal.

The new guy was known as a passing guru, a longtime NFL assistant who had nurtured Joe Montana and Danny White. "The thing that Paul spends a lot of time on is detail, probably more so than anybody I have been associated with," Montana once said. Hackett was something of a mad scientist, able to converse at length about the finer points of the passing game, always wearing wire-rimmed glasses and a ball cap tugged down over his forehead. It was not difficult to imagine him staying up late at night, working under a desk lamp, wildly sketching plays on a notepad.

He arrived at USC the same time as Palmer, the big, blond kid from Orange County who was hailed as a savior before so much as stepping foot on campus. Late in their first season together, the freshman strong-armed his way into the starting lineup and led the team to three victories in four games. Then things turned sour. USC lost to underdog Texas Christian in the 1998 Sun Bowl. The next season, Palmer broke his collarbone trying to bull past a defender at Oregon, and the team limped home to a 6–6 record.

So the victory over Penn State was vital. It did not take a scientist to figure out that, entering his third season with a very mediocre 14–11 record, Hackett needed to produce a winner. "We've had an opportunity to do some groundwork for two years," he said. "We were disappointed in our won-loss record last year, but we're ready to make a significant jump."

The Trojans returned to the Coliseum and sneaked past Colorado, winning 17–14 on a field goal with 13 seconds remaining. The next week, they overcame a halftime deficit against San Jose State to win, 34–24. Heading into the Pac-10 schedule, USC had risen all the way to No. 8 in the nation, and fans were speculating about a return to the good old days. Behind the scenes, however, the coaches quietly worried.

That game against Colorado should not have been so close. And there had been too many dropped passes, too many penalties, versus San Jose State. Brent McCaffrey, a senior on the offensive line, had sounded the first warning note when he said, "I guess you could say we deserved to lose."

———

That fall, Hackett knew he was not the first USC coach to feel the heat, not by a long shot. "The nature of USC football is that we expect to be the best," he said. "There's always going to be that." He was referring to a tradition that predated his arrival on campus by a century.

The university, built on mustard fields south of downtown Los Angeles, fielded its first team in 1888. The early seasons were not much to speak of, less than a handful of games each fall against opponents such as the Alliance Athletic Club, Chaffey College, and Cal Tech. Not until 1904 did the school hire its first salaried coach, Harvey Holmes, and not until 1923 did USC begin playing in the newly built Los Angeles Memorial Coliseum. Maybe the biggest thing to come out of those years was a nickname. According to a history compiled by the late Mal Florence, a *Los Angeles Times* sportswriter named Owen R. Bird decided that because the fledgling program continually played larger and better-equipped opponents, "Trojans" would be a fitting moniker.

The rise of USC football truly began in 1919 with the hiring of Elmer Henderson as coach. During his six seasons, "Gloomy Gus" constantly downplayed his team's chances in the newspapers, even as he employed the relatively new technique of recruiting to stockpile his roster with all the best local athletes. The Trojans amassed a record of 45–7 under his guidance and went to their first Rose Bowl, defeating Penn State 14–3 on New Year's Day, 1923. About the only thing Henderson could not do was defeat rival California, which led to his firing in 1924. The stage was set for the birth of a national power.

Looking for someone to lead the team, USC tried to hire legendary Knute Rockne away from Notre Dame and, by various accounts, nearly succeeded. When the Irish persuaded their coach to stay put, the Trojans turned to a former All-American from Yale named Howard Jones. What Jones might have lacked in name recognition, he made up in sheer willpower. "Very intense," former quarterback Ambrose Schindler said. "Everything was football. All his thoughts were about football."

The game was different then, the ball almost as fat and round as a rugby ball, the players staying on the field for offense and defense, no face masks. Jones preached a straight-ahead attack that featured the quarterback running out of a single-wing formation. An occasional pass or wingback reverse found its way into the mix, but such was Jones' determination to pound the ball downfield that his teams became known as the "Thundering Herd." The Trojans soon barged their way to the top of the national rankings with a succession of All-Americans, including Mort Kaer, Morley Drury, Cotton Warburton, and Grenny Lansdell—names woven into the fabric of the school's athletic history. Through the late twenties and early thirties, USC became a worthy rival to Notre Dame and won several championships.

The first came in 1928, when a scoreless tie with Cal was the only blemish on a 9–0–1 record that featured dominating victories over opponents such as Pop Warner's squad at Stanford. Three years later, the Trojans lost their opener to St. Mary's but went undefeated the rest of the way. They upset Notre Dame in South Bend on Johnny Baker's last-minute field goal and later beat Tulane in the Rose Bowl to wrap up a second title. The team won so much, Schindler said, because of its coach's unwavering attention to detail, his insistence that players be precise. Once, against the Irish, a Trojan defender lined up "six inches wider than Howard Jones wanted him," Schindler recalled. "The runner broke inside and went 60 yards for a touchdown. That's how exact the coach was . . . and we had to do things his way or we didn't play."

Jones would have two more great teams. The 1932 squad went undefeated, surrendering only 13 points all season, beating Pittsburgh, 35–0, in the Rose Bowl. The 1939 Trojans were tied twice but never lost, earning the No. 1 spot in one poll by defeating No. 2 Tennessee, 14–0, in Pasadena. It was the last hurrah for Jones, who left after the next season and soon died of a heart attack at age 55.

All of this might have seemed like ancient history in the fall of 2000, but memories of the old championships still fluttered around the Coliseum, the ghost of the old coach and the heritage he helped to create making their presence felt. The media guide still featured black-and-white snapshots of the Thundering Herd. As former lineman Carl Benson put it, "Just so many good football players."

Hackett knew what he was up against.

———

The 2000 season began to fall apart at Oregon State. USC had not lost to the Beavers since 1967, a remarkable stretch of 26 consecutive victories, so the fans who packed into tiny Reser Stadium in Corvallis that afternoon were raucous and angry, eager for revenge.

They grew increasingly loud as the game wore on, their underdog team staying close through a tense first half. At the start of the third quarter, the Trojans had a chance to seize control, Palmer throwing for a go-ahead touchdown on fourth-and-1. But a yellow flag lay on the turf. Delay of game. Hackett later took the blame, saying that he had waited too long before sending in the play, musing, "It all comes down to that drive."

Set five yards back, the Trojans chose to try a field goal and watched as the kick bounced off an upright. They never quite recovered. Tailback Petros Papadakis fumbled early in the fourth quarter, and Palmer threw a costly interception, his third of the night. Soon after, Oregon State running back Ken Simonton, who had been piling up yardage all game, broke loose for a 36-yard touchdown to give his team a 31–21 lead. In the final seconds, the fans chanted, "It's all over," then swarmed the field to celebrate the end of the streak.

"Maybe this will open some players' eyes," said USC's fiercely competitive linebacker Zeke Moreno, after dodging his way to the locker room. "Now we really have to fight." But back in Los Angeles, he remained troubled by something that had happened in the second quarter, when he scooped up a fumble and ran 80 yards for a touchdown. "Guys should have been all over me," Moreno said. They weren't. "You could tell the emotion wasn't there."

The next few weeks played out like a recurring nightmare. At home against Arizona, a sleepy-looking USC defense gave up three quick touchdowns, and Palmer had three more interceptions, which led to scattered boos from the same Coliseum crowd that had cheered the team through earlier victories. "There's not a whole lot to say," Hackett grumbled after the 31–15 defeat. Next came a 28–17 loss to Oregon. Then a trip to Stanford ended in heartbreak, the Cardinal winning on a 20-yard touchdown pass with no time remaining. "It seems like everybody has something on us," Palmer said. "Some luck or some magic."

The truth was, the Trojans had only themselves to blame. Every week brought the same thing: breakdowns on defense and special teams, offside by the offensive line for no reason. Kareem Kelly, the speedy wide receiver, had a habit of dropping passes, and Palmer kept making mistakes by trying to do too much. After a 28–16 loss to Cal, a dispirited performance that extended the losing streak to five games, Kelly told reporters, "Just use my answers from last week."

The team had long since slipped from the national rankings, all that excited talk about a Rose Bowl replaced by "Fire Hackett" grumblings. The coach went about his work as usual, but players spoke of being distracted by the rumors. Mike Garrett, the former Heisman-winning tailback who now served as athletic director, called the losing "unbearable" and said, "Your nerves get frayed." When asked about Hackett's job security, he repeated the same line over and over: *The matter would be reviewed at season's end.*

"I have to be fair to everyone involved," he said. "But I must tell you, it hurts."

No one hurt more than the seniors: Moreno and Papadakis, defensive lineman Ennis Davis and center Eric Denmon. They had come to USC expecting a bowl game—if not a trip to Pasadena—at the end of each season. Instead, they got fans and classmates opining about every little thing that went wrong. "Even my friends call and talk about specific plays and why we didn't do this or that," Papadakis said. The players felt the tug of history, backup quarterback Mike Van Raaphorst explained, "You'd like to leave a better legacy."

––––––––

The modern era at USC began in 1960 when a little-known assistant named John McKay took over as head coach. Much like Jones so many years before him, McKay had specific, if updated, notions about how to run an offense. He began tinkering with a modified I formation that put the tailback seven yards behind the line of scrimmage, affording the runner a wide view of the play as it unfolded. This scheme took a while to perfect, his teams struggling for a couple of seasons before turning the corner in 1962.

That fall, the Trojans featured not only a pair of skilled quarterbacks in Pete Beathard and Bill Nelsen, but also a defense that limited opponents to a touchdown or less in eight games. Their 10–0 regular season included a tough win against UCLA and a shutout of Notre Dame. Then, in the Rose Bowl, they withstood a fierce rally by Wisconsin, hanging on for a 42–37 victory and the first national championship since the Jones era.

The next fall, Mike Garrett arrived on campus. At that time, he said, McKay wanted the I formation to feature the quarterback. If so, the coach was persuaded otherwise as his new tailback set an NCAA career-rushing record with 3,221 yards in three seasons and, in 1965, became only the second West Coast player to win the Heisman Trophy. Although Garrett's very good teams always fell just short of the Rose Bowl, his powerful running set the standard for a program that would eventually become known as Tailback U.

Over the next decade, a parade of talented ball carriers led USC to seven Rose Bowls and three more national championships. This royal procession included another Heisman winner, O. J. Simpson, and a player who many believe should have won, Anthony Davis. Along the way, McKay became legendary for both his football smarts and a lightning-quick wit.

Talking about the value of emotion, he said, "Emotion is overrated. My wife is emotional, but she's a lousy football player."

On the subject of intensity: "Intensity is a lot of guys who run fast."

Asked why Simpson carried the ball so much, he answered, "Why not? It isn't very heavy. Besides, he doesn't belong to a union."

The 1967 season provided another classic one-liner. Minutes before kickoff at Notre Dame Stadium in South Bend, McKay refused to bring his players out of the locker room. His reasoning was simple: two years earlier, Notre Dame had kept them waiting outside in chilly weather and the Trojans had lost badly. Now, McKay vowed not to not budge until the Irish took the field. The referee threatened to call the game.

"What does that mean?" McKay asked.

"It means Notre Dame wins, 2–0, on a forfeit."

The coach replied, "That would be the best damn deal we've ever gotten in this stadium."

McKay's final years in college football would be among his best. His undefeated 1972 squad, featuring fullback Sam "Bam" Cunningham, tight end Charles Young, and linebacker Richard Wood, ranked with the greatest of all time, never trailing in the second half of any game and demolishing Ohio State, 42–17, in the Rose Bowl. The Trojans became the first team to receive every first-place vote in both the Associated Press and United Press International polls.

Two years later, another powerful USC squad found itself trailing Notre Dame, 24–0, at the Coliseum. "The Comeback"—now a part of school lore—began simply enough, with a Davis touchdown and a missed two-point conversion to make the score 24–6 at halftime. In the locker room, an unruffled McKay told his players, "They're going to kick the ball to [Davis], and he's going to bring it all the way back." The tailback figured that his coach had gone crazy but, sure enough, he returned the second-half kickoff 102 yards for a touchdown and ignited an offensive frenzy. In all, USC scored 55 points in a dizzying 17 minutes for a 55–24 victory. As Davis put it, "We turned into madmen."

The ensuing Rose Bowl proved just as thrilling, with quarterback Pat Haden throwing a fourth-quarter touchdown pass to the coach's son, J. K. McKay, then completing a two-point conversion to Shelton Diggs for an 18–17 win over Ohio State. Although the Trojans had started the season with a loss, the victory propelled them to their fourth and final national championship of the McKay era.

If fans were concerned about a letdown after McKay left to coach the Tampa Bay Buccaneers in 1976, their fears were soon calmed.

Conquest

The team brought back a former assistant named John Robinson, who continued the tradition of Tailback U. by nurturing Ricky Bell and Heisman winners Charles White and Marcus Allen. Robinson won three Rose Bowls in his first four seasons and added another national championship trophy to the Heritage Hall lobby in 1978.

It seemed as if the USC dynasty might never end.

When Petros Papadakis was a boy, the USC football team often ate dinner at his family's restaurant, Papadakis Taverna, something of a landmark in the port town of San Pedro. "I would walk around and get the guys to autograph a menu," he said. "I lived and died with every game." His father and older brother had played for the Trojans, and Petros eventually followed in their footsteps.

But by the time he arrived at USC in the midnineties, things had changed. Robinson, back for a second term, was soon fired. How much farther did the team sink under Hackett? In that disastrous 2000 season, the players were walking off the field after losing to Cal when Papadakis heard someone shout his name. He glanced toward the seats around the tunnel, where fans often congregated to ask for autographs. A man yelled an obscenity, Papadakis said, "and then he threw a bottle at me."

That was nothing compared to the animosity directed at the coach. His special teams continued to falter no matter how often he changed practice routines and strategies. His relationship with offensive coordinator Hue Jackson was deteriorating, sources within the team said. The men disagreed over strategy, often during games, while Palmer waited for a play to come in from the sideline. No matter who made the call, fans believed the Trojans were too conservative, running instead of throwing the ball, punting instead of gambling on fourth down. And Hackett's blitzing defense kept getting burned.

The coach began to second-guess himself, wondering if he should abandon the run and rely more heavily on his encyclopedic knowledge of the passing game. Although his tailback, McCullough, was having a decent enough season, other teams in the conference kept blowing past with high-powered aerial attacks. "That probably should have told me something," Hackett said. "The nights when you don't sleep—and I haven't for three weeks—you're thinking about exactly that kind of thing."

By late November, the atmosphere around the 4–6 Trojans resembled nothing so much as a death watch. The players tried to keep up a brave front, with fullback Charlie Landrigan telling reporters that while "a lot of teams would go in the tank . . . we've tried to block it out." But behind the scenes, "the whole thing began to unravel," said Papadakis, who later became a radio and television commentator. "There were no leaders on the team to handle it. It was just a matter of getting through the year."

The Trojans had one last gasp in them, a moment to celebrate, against UCLA. Playing at the Rose Bowl, they suffered all the usual mishaps—a fumble in the end zone, more than a dozen penalties, more play-calling problems—only this time Palmer compensated with the best night of his career, passing for 350 yards and four touchdowns. With the score tied and nine seconds remaining, David Bell, who had begun the season as a third-string kicker, wobbled a 36-yard field goal through the uprights for a 38–35 victory. Hackett rushed across the field, past swarms of reporters and players, toward the end of the stadium where the USC fans sat. Waving the band director, the venerated Arthur C. Bartner, out of the way, he climbed the conductor's ladder and flashed a victory sign at the crowd. The same fans who had taunted him after losses, who had called for his head, now responded with cheers. But the question remained: Would it be enough to save his job?

Rumors swirled during the next seven days. USC had an option to buy out the final two years on Hackett's five-year contract for $800,000, and Oregon State's Dennis Erickson was mentioned as a possible replacement. So was Mike Riley, the popular San Diego Chargers coach with strong ties to the program. Some players voiced their support for Hackett, asking that Garrett give him a vote of confidence. Others remained silent.

"A lot of guys want him back," explained Kelly, the receiver. "There's also a lot of guys who don't care."

The season finale against No. 11 Notre Dame was a kind of slow funeral march. Starting with a few minutes left in the third quarter, the Irish ran the ball 24 straight times. Twenty-four times spanning four possessions, two touchdowns, a field goal and, ultimately, a 38–21 victory. Palmer threw two more interceptions, tying the school record for 18 in a season, putting the defense in difficult situations. A pained Garrett walked out of the locker room, saying, "I've got to deliberate and make a decision."

Sitting before a roomful of reporters, Hackett talked like a man who wanted to stick around, already looking forward to spring practice and fixing the problems that had bedeviled his team. Someone asked him if he deserved to keep his job. "Are you out of your mind?" he bristled. "Of course I do." Later, in a calmer tone, he said, "I'm going to take a few more questions. Then I'm going to hibernate."

For the first time in school history, USC finished last in the conference. But it wasn't just the disappointment of this particular season. A 5–7 record, yet another mediocre finish, served to reinforce a now-familiar refrain. Opponents no longer feared the Trojans. Blue-chip recruits no longer desired them. They might never be dominant again.

CHAPTER 3

"A Big Choice"

Things had not gone smoothly, to say the least, when USC fired John Robinson in 1997. Mike Garrett kept him around for several weeks after a 6–5 season, even as news reports had the athletic director speaking with various candidates. When the decision finally came down, Garrett said he called Robinson several times and left messages that were not returned, which led to a bizarre day.

Garrett and university President Steven Sample met with reporters at Heritage Hall to announce the firing. Several miles north, at a downtown hotel, Robinson held a separate news conference, claiming that he and his assistants had been "hung out to dry" and that he had learned of his ouster secondhand. Alumni were sympathetic to the longtime coach. Awkward weeks had passed before Paul Hackett, the offensive coordinator for the Kansas City Chiefs, finished with the NFL playoffs and arrived on campus.

Three years later, with Hackett on the hot seat, Garrett was being more cautious. "I want to protect everyone's interests—the football team, the coaches, the alumni—and make the right decision," he said. It did not take long. The Monday after the loss to Notre Dame, Hackett drove to campus at 6:45 A.M., knowing that he was gone. He spoke with his assistants first, then consulted with an athletic department official about how to handle the announcement. By midmorning, 20 or so reporters were ushered into an upstairs office where, under normal circumstances, the coaching staff would gather to watch film. Entering the room moments later, Hackett quipped, "Where's the executioner's chair?"

The meeting soon turned serious. "For someone who has given three years of his life, and for the last six months hasn't slept or eaten, I'm very disappointed," Hackett said. "I'm disappointed we don't get a chance to continue this and complete this. I felt things were headed in the right direction." He added, "There's no question we took our lumps this year." Later, he sat in his office with a handful of beat writers and columnists who had been with the team on a daily basis. Gracious and poised, he chatted for several minutes before leaving the building through a side door, waving away television crews that had waited outside.

It was left to Garrett to face the cameras. He said Hackett had done "some nice things for USC," yet made clear his belief that the players "weren't progressing, weren't developing" and added, "All of us have gone through a lot of pain, a lot of suffering. When we don't beat people, it's painful." As for finding someone new, the Trojans were not interested in an up-and-coming assistant, he said. They wanted a leader with a track record as a head coach, preferably in the college ranks, though the NFL was not ruled out. Garrett acknowledged that he had received calls from several interested parties and spoke of coaches he respected, including Wisconsin's Barry Alvarez and the San Diego Chargers' Mike Riley. Asked about Dennis Erickson, he replied, "I think he is someone I should look up." In fact, USC was already negotiating with Erickson.

The Oregon State coach was a hot commodity. He had coached in college and the pros and knew the Pac-10 well, having revived the woeful Beavers in only a few years, leading them to a 10–1 record and a share of the conference title that very season. USC officials thought they were "well down the road" to an agreement with him, Daryl Gross, a senior associate athletic director, said years later. Sources put the deal at $7.2 million over five years.

"A Big Choice"

In the best of worlds, the hiring would have been announced within a couple of days, the transition swift and seamless. But Erickson balked. His assistants weren't sure they wanted to live in Los Angeles, and his current employer was offering a lucrative contract extension. "We have no intention of giving up on what I think is an outstanding coach and coaching staff," said Mitch Barnhart, the Oregon State athletic director. If USC was going to find someone to lead its football team to better days, the process would not be so easy.

———

Coming out of Roosevelt High as a prep All-American in the early sixties, Mike Garrett was all set to play for UCLA. Except the Bruins were not sure they wanted him. "They thought I was too small," he said many years later. "They asked me to go to junior college." At the last moment, John McKay offered him a scholarship to USC.

The kid from East Los Angeles arrived on campus with grand, if somewhat vague, ambitions. "I didn't know what I wanted to be. I just wanted to be successful," he said. He was good enough at baseball to play outfield for the Trojans and eventually be drafted by the Pittsburgh Pirates and Los Angeles Dodgers, but it did not take long for McKay or anyone else to realize that his true talent was running the football. Not only did Garrett set more than a dozen NCAA, conference, and school records during his career, he might have altered the course of the program.

The Trojans had just won a national championship with an offense that featured quarterbacks Pete Beathard and Bill Nelsen, so the I formation was geared toward the pass. According to Garrett, when Beathard and Nelsen graduated, McKay had to rely on the tailback position and soon discovered that talented runners were more plentiful than quarterbacks. Thus began a USC tradition.

Conquest

Not long after accepting the Heisman Trophy in 1965, Garrett signed with the Kansas City Chiefs and the next season returned to the Coliseum to face his boyhood idols, the Green Bay Packers, in Super Bowl I. "One thing I always loved about USC was that it prepared you for everything in life," he told the *Los Angeles Times* in a 1993 interview. "'SC is not designed to make you happy or make you perfect—it is designed to prepare you for reality. I was fully prepared to play against my heroes."

His NFL career lasted eight years, including another trip to the Super Bowl and 1,000-yard seasons with the Chiefs and the Chargers. Life after football brought a series of management positions in business, campaigns for Congress and San Diego City Council in the early eighties, then a law degree from Western State University College of Law. In 1990, Garrett was considering the purchase of a lucrative beer distributorship when Mike McGee, the USC athletic director, called him.

"He had some issues that needed to be dealt with," Garrett said. "Mike asked me to come back."

Garrett returned to the university as an associate athletic director and, many assumed, McGee's handpicked successor, but there was hesitation when McGee announced that he was leaving three years later. Certain alumni did not like Garrett. He was seen as serious, demanding, sometimes warm and other times gruff. "People thought there might be a better man for the job," he said. A search committee considered several candidates, including basketball coach George Raveling, before selecting the former tailback. At a January 1993 news conference, Sample told the assembled crowd, "Mike Garrett not only knows the great Trojan athletic tradition, he helped create it." The 48-year-old Garrett, still possessing a powerful build, the determined look of an athlete, fought back tears as he stood at the podium that day.

"A Big Choice"

"There has been no prouder moment than this for me," he said. "I came here in 1962, and we have been through a lot—a lot of good, a lot of indifferent. But you know the amazing thing about it, it's still great to be a Trojan."

The next eight years saw one impressive accomplishment after another. USC won national championships in baseball, tennis, and swimming. Fundraising reached record heights, graduation rates increased, and the department, which had come under pressure from equal rights groups, added two women's sports. Yet, from the very start, Garrett knew that "the whole catch at our place is to win national championships in football." The Trojans had amassed a less-than-sparkling record of 56–39–2 during his tenure. It had been his decision to fire Robinson. His decision to hire Hackett. Now, some in the media suggested, Garrett's next choice would go a long way toward shaping his legacy.

Peculiar forces come into play when a football program goes looking for a coach. Athletic directors prefer to move quickly and quietly, which might involve using intermediaries, secret phone calls, private jets flown to clandestine meetings. If all goes smoothly, no one knows until the day the hiring is announced. Things rarely go that smoothly. Reporters are always hovering, impatient to feed information to fans who want to know every step of the process. Sometimes the candidates themselves throw a wrench in the machinery. A coach being considered for a job might leak information to the media because he likes the prestige that comes with being sought after or because he wants leverage in renegotiating a contract with his current employer. Add to this volatile mix the pressure of time.

Conquest

As the Trojans conducted their search in the late fall of 2000, the clock was ticking, roughly two months remaining until the day they could officially sign high school recruits. Like other prospects, Matt Leinart had verbally committed to Hackett, but now Hackett was gone. The Mater Dei High quarterback found himself in limbo, waiting to see who the Trojans would hire, suddenly considering a trip to Oklahoma. "Believe me," Bob Stoops would later say, "it was down to us and 'SC." The Trojans needed to get a staff in place and hit the recruiting trail.

Erickson was still wavering and negotiating with Oregon State, so USC drew up contingency plans. As Garrett's chief advisor on coaching searches, Gross had a wish list of names, check marks for various categories with an emphasis on defensive expertise and head-coaching experience. Sonny Lubick of Colorado State was on the list. So was Mike Bellotti, the highly respected coach at Oregon.

The Ducks ranked among the top programs in the nation and had defeated USC in each of the previous three seasons. In late November, athletic department officials secretly met with Bellotti and subsequently spoke with his two agents. The coach said only, "I can tell you honestly I have been contacted by several schools in the past week about whether I'd be interested. They've talked, I've listened, and that is as far as anything has gone." A sports Internet site reported that the Trojans offered him $1.6 million a year plus incentives, but Gross later insisted their discussions never progressed beyond the preliminary stages.

In early December, another name surfaced: Pete Carroll. USC had approached him about the job once before, when Robinson was fired, but now he seemed an unlikely candidate. He had not coached in the college ranks since the early eighties, and his 33–31 record with the New York Jets and New England Patriots was hardly overwhelming. There was another problem. "Paul Hackett was an experience that did not go well," Gross said years later. "So the populace was saying 'You can't bring another pro coach in here.' That automatically made Pete not the first choice."

Besides, USC was still pursuing Erickson and Bellotti. As it turned out, the school would get neither of them. Bellotti soon announced his intention to sign a contract extension through 2007 for roughly $1 million a year. He called the decision "very difficult, the most difficult of my life." Erickson got a new deal too, agreeing to stay at Oregon State for a potential $7 million over seven years.

"Good for him," Garrett said when reporters found the athletic director in the stands at a basketball game. "Otherwise, no comment."

No less than a dozen major colleges were looking for coaches after the 2000 season, big-time programs such as Brigham Young, Maryland, and Oklahoma State. Within the Pac-10, Arizona and Arizona State had openings to fill. Even Alabama, with its hallowed history, had failed to lure Butch Davis away from Miami. It was a seller's market, a tough time to be shopping.

Around USC, each passing day brought more questions. At the start of the search, Garrett had assured fans that he was hearing from a number of "reputable" coaches interested in the job. "We're still 'SC with a great tradition," he said. So why was it taking this long? Was tradition—all those trophies in the Heritage Hall lobby—enough?

Certainly not everyone wanted to live in Los Angeles. Bellotti had talked about the benefits of a small college town where his kids could ride their bicycles to watch afternoon practice. "It comes down to what you think is best for you and your family," he said. Erickson had made similar allusions to Corvallis. And with other Pac-10 schools spending tens of millions on construction, USC had fallen behind in the facilities race. The Coliseum was rapidly aging, and the practice field seemed cramped and gloomy, wedged between the remodeled baseball stadium and a modern Olympic swimming pool. Even Heritage Hall was showing wear around the edges. It had been built in 1971, when the athletic department had fewer teams, and, despite improvements, was packed to capacity, boxes stacked along walls.

"It's a mediocre job," a rival coach told Chris Dufresne of the *Los Angeles Times*. "No one has come to grips with the 10- to 12-year non-investment in the program."

Even more daunting were certain alumni and fans still living in the McKay era. Hackett had warned as much on his way out the door. "I love the passion and tradition and expectations, but c'mon," he said. "People around here need to realize, when it comes to football, it's a new world out there. A new era. A new landscape." Scholarship limits had leveled the playing field, preventing large programs from stockpiling talent, and tougher academic standards were keeping some kids out of school. Leigh Steinberg, the well-known agent who represented Hackett, said, "Anybody advising a coach would have to bring that up. You have to be realistic." Still, Garrett remained adamant that he could attract a top name. Behind the scenes, Gross also preached patience, saying that the search was proceeding step by step, with everything under control.

Upbeat, often wisecracking, Gross was a distinctive presence in the athletic department offices, a counterbalance to his more somber boss. He had grown up in Beverly Hills and gone off to play football at UC-Davis, where as a receiver he caught passes from future Jets quarterback Ken O'Brien. After his playing days, he coached at Davis for a while before eventually coming to USC to work as a graduate assistant and earn his Ph.D. in educational psychology. Garrett hired him as an assistant athletic director in 1991, and Gross had quickly worked his way up the ladder. By 2000, nine sports came under his purview, as well as the department's academic and drug-testing programs. But nothing put him in the spotlight more than his role in coaching searches.

Anyone wondering what USC might do next could have found a clue in his résumé. From 1988 to 1990, Gross had left the university to work as an NFL scout. His team? The Jets. The defensive coordinator during his last year there? Carroll.

———

By the second week of December, the public's attention had shifted to Mike Riley in San Diego. He was beloved by players and media alike for his affable nature. Although he had suffered through losing seasons with the Chargers and at Oregon State, Riley was generally credited with starting the Beavers in the right direction—laying the groundwork for Erickson's success—and had guided the Winnipeg Blue Bombers to a pair of championships in the Canadian Football League. Equally important, he had served as an assistant to Robinson and knew the Trojan heritage.

"I loved 'SC," he said. "I grew up a Pac-10 gym rat and saw all the games. It was a privilege to get to go there and coach."

There was one hang up: the Chargers had him under contract for three more years and seemed in no mood to let him walk away. "We have not been contacted and, if we are, we will deny permission to talk to Mike," a team spokesman said. In fact, Riley was already in discussions with USC. He was also in a tricky spot. On one hand, he had to wonder if the Trojans were truly willing to haggle with San Diego to get him out of his contract. On the other, with the Chargers a dismal 1–12, he must have worried that team officials—despite their protestations—might end up firing him anyway. On December 9, after meeting with team president Dean Spanos, Riley had neither an offer from USC nor any guarantee of remaining with the Chargers.

In the meantime, Carroll had flown from his Massachusetts home for an interview that, unknown to the outside world, had gone extraordinarily well. "Pete was just so amazingly engaging," Gross said. "His enthusiasm and his energy mixed with his expertise." Garrett listened to his concise plan for rebuilding the team and thought, *Oh my God, this guy's a home run.* Sticking around Los Angeles for several days, Carroll watched the USC women's volleyball team, which happened to include his daughter Jaime, win a regional final in the NCAA playoffs. He also turned up on the sideline at a Saturday night championship game between two local high schools, Long Beach Poly and Loyola. USC tight end Antoine Harris and cornerback Darrell Rideaux were standing on the sideline that night.

"He walked up and introduced himself," Harris said. "We talked a little while."

Another candidate was in town around the same time. Sonny Lubick had been highly successful at Colorado State and had prior experience as a Stanford assistant, so he knew the Pacific-10. But he came away from his meeting with USC officials feeling as if he would not get a return call. By then, Gross said, the choice had come down to Riley or Carroll, with Carroll holding an edge, in large part, because of that knockout interview. Reached at his home, Carroll sounded hopeful. "There has been strong mutual interest," he said. "It's a pretty hot topic right now. I'm looking forward to seeing what the outcome is."

The university soon brought him back for a second interview, and his father, Jim, said, "He had the idea it was all set. He was very excited about the possibility." Carroll was so optimistic that he called former Trojan and NFL defensive back Ronnie Lott. "He wanted to make sure he had a feel for the school," Lott said. "He wanted to know what I recalled about it, what made it special." But as negotiations moved toward a deal, there was still time for the turmoil, if not outright madness, that can accompany a coaching search.

"I remember at one point having Pete on the phone and, on hold, was Mike Riley," Gross said. "That's what happens in those things. I'm like, what if Pete drops out? I need to have my next guy."

On the afternoon of December 13, a sports Internet site ran a story that the Trojans were set to hire Carroll. Then, within an hour, a San Diego television station reported that the Chargers were going to fire Riley, which in turn led to speculation that *he* was headed for USC. Emerging from a long staff meeting, Riley heard about all this from his wife. "She asked me if I'd been fired," he told a San Diego radio station. "That was the first I'd heard of it. I thought she was kidding." Carroll, laying low in Southern California, kept track of all this through newspapers and radio. He recalled listening to "all the dialogue and all that about Mike [Garrett] trying to make a decision and the choices they were looking at. I mean, I knew a lot more than the people who were talking."

The San Diego television station quickly retracted its report about Riley's firing and, the next day, word spread that USC was close to giving Carroll a contract, which sparked a new round of commotion. According to various reports, alumni bombarded the athletic department with telephone calls and e-mails, convinced Garrett was making a mistake. USC supposedly scheduled a news conference, then backed off because of the angry reaction. One newspaper story had Sample, the university president, stepping in. Another hinted at renewed negotiations with Riley.

Carroll was partly amused, partly anxious. "There was a time when I felt like they were going to offer me the job but still waited a couple of days," he said. "Those couple of days were very painful because the media was way off what was going to happen. I thought, 'Put an end to this.'"

Conquest

———

On the morning of December 15, nearly three weeks after the search had begun, USC called a news conference to introduce Carroll as its new coach. Though financial terms were not disclosed, sources put his initial salary at approximately $1 million a year. Reporters and television cameras crowded into a lounge on the ground floor of Heritage Hall, a room with a podium up front and more-formal furniture, upholstered in school colors, to one side. University staff and fans pushed in, too.

Before the proceedings began, athletic department officials made the rounds, talking to the media about giving Carroll a fair shake. A public relations firm had contacted reporters on his behalf, and former USC players such as Lott and Willie McGinest were voicing their support. "His energy suits college guys," McGinest said. Clearly, everyone knew this hiring would generate controversy. The *Los Angeles Times* sports section was already receiving dozens of angry e-mails, a sampling of which were published in the next day's paper.

"Mike Garrett, what was it about Pete Carroll that made you want to hire him for the head coaching job? Was it his lifetime record of two games over .500? His complete lack of recruiting ties to the West Coast? His limited college coaching experience? His reputation for being soft on players and not a good motivator?"

And.

"It doesn't take a rocket scientist to realize that this appears to be a net loss, but then Mike Garrett is not a rocket scientist. A rocket scientist would at least make sure the rocket was pointed up, not down, before lighting the fuse."

And.

"How long until we have to buy out Carroll's contract?"

The coach at the center of this tempest recalled, simply, "The reaction was not a great reaction." Carroll had been in this position before. People questioned his lack of experience when he took over the Jets in 1994 and doubted his pedigree when he replaced the immensely popular Bill Parcells in New England in 1997. Having endured those ordeals, he knew what had to be done. "I needed to get to that first press conference because they were really after me," he said. "That was my first challenge."

Dressed in a dark suit with a red tie, Carroll stood before the microphones and made a case for himself. "I've been an unpopular choice in the past," he said. "What it is, it's a challenge." He insisted that his long absence from the college game would not be a problem, that recruiting wasn't so much different from evaluating talent for the NFL draft. He talked about his belief in aggressive defense, attacking the ball, creating turnovers, while also addressing concerns about USC's offense. "Wide open, spread the field, use the space, calling on the athletic ability of your players," he said. "That's what we have to do to win the Pac-10." To many, he appeared confident and animated, gesturing, pacing. Some thought he looked uneasy. The television cameramen were not exactly thrilled, having to follow each move.

Later, as Carroll did one-on-one interviews, Garrett mused that "anytime you have to make a big choice, you get kind of nervous." He also let the slightest bit of irritation show, saying that criticism of the search and his decision had been inappropriately personal, adding that "the Joe Blow doesn't know football." Gross, in keeping with his nature, took a more enthusiastic approach, working the room, his words fast and excited.

"Believe me, I understand the public opinion," the assistant said. "But if you ask people in the industry of football, 99 percent of them would say Pete Carroll knows football. I feel like that guy who says, 'Come see it, if you don't like it, I'll give you your money back.'"

CHAPTER 4

An Unconventional Approach

Only four seasons later, the controversy that had marked Pete Carroll's hiring seemed like ancient history The week before the 2005 Orange Bowl, fans waited for him to walk through the lobby at the team hotel, and bowl executives wanted him for promotional appearances. There were autographs to sign. Endless interview requests. He looked good on camera—he was still youthful at 53 and had an eagerness in his voice and that perpetual tan.

Asked if it felt like sweet revenge, Carroll frowned. "I don't think that way."

Afternoon practice had just ended. The coach was making his way toward a jumble of lights and cameras, the television crews waiting for their daily fix. He paused beside one of the big Orange Bowl buses with his likeness seven feet tall on the side and considered the question again. Wasn't he tempted—even just a little—to say "I told you so" to the people who had doubted him back in 2000?

"I think people had a pretty good opinion," he said. "They only went with what they knew. They didn't know any better."

They did not know the boy who grew up in Greenbrae, a suburb just outside of San Francisco. Sports came naturally to him, but he wasn't as big as the other kids. Around the time he reached high school, Carroll read a magazine article about basketball player Rick Barry, who said something along the lines of, "I'm a lifetime 46 percent shooter, so if I miss my first 10 shots, watch out." The brazen confidence of that quote struck a chord. Rather than grow discouraged or carry a chip on his shoulder, Carroll chose to believe that one day he would get a chance to prove himself. "A little guy barely making the team," said Dave Perron, a friend and former teammate, "Peter was really a late bloomer. A lot of people were surprised at how good he was."

Despite his size, Carroll starred in football, basketball, and baseball at Redwood High and, as a senior, was the school's athlete of the year. A stint at junior college gave his body more time to catch up, got him noticed by coaches at the University of the Pacific in nearby Stockton, where he became a starter in the secondary. Even then, his approach to the game was unconventional. A team photograph shows a young man wearing jersey No. 46, his hair long and dark, a gleeful look in his eyes. While other players at Pacific spent the minutes before kickoff in predictable fashion—some quietly grim; others rowdy, butting helmets—Carroll and Perron slipped off to the sideline. "Peter and I just threw the ball around," Perron said. "We had fun." If this attitude seemed quirky, it was difficult to argue with the results; Carroll earned all-conference honors as a safety in 1971 and 1972.

"You think he's a happy-go-lucky guy?" asked Walt Harris, a member of the Pacific staff who later coached Pittsburgh and Stanford. "Well, he would knock you out. He would hurt you and love it."

After college, Carroll took a shot at the pros, an unsuccessful tryout with the World Football League, and briefly sold building materials. His college coach, Chester Caddas, ran into his parents one day and asked about him. They said he was thinking about getting into coaching. "If he's willing to work for nothing, we can give him a place to sleep and meals," Caddas said. "Tell him to show up next week." Carroll did, returning to Pacific to join the football staff and study for a graduate degree in physical education. No one who knew him was surprised.

"Even when he was playing Pop Warner he was always down on a knee diagramming plays in the dirt," said Bob Troppman, his coach at Redwood High. "His mind was always going. When I think of Pete, he's always sort of running. All the time moving."

———

Pacific was a good place to learn the nuances of the game. A small independent university, it had been home to the legendary Amos Alonzo Stagg in the forties and, after that, had produced a startling number of high-profile coaches for such a minor football program. Tom Flores played quarterback for the Tigers in the fifties. Jon Gruden and Mike Martz, Buddy Ryan and Bob Toledo—all of them worked on the staff at some point.

The seventies—when Carroll returned for graduate school—were also a time of exploration in sport. People were looking at the jock world in new ways, delving beyond the merely physical, examining connections between mind and body. Tim Gallwey broke ground with his best-selling book, *The Inner Game of Tennis*, drawing upon Zen philosophy and other diverse elements to help athletes stay focused. At Esalen, the Big Sur institute devoted to the human potential movement, cofounder Michael Murphy was developing his ideas about transcendent experiences in sport.

All of this intrigued Carroll because it sought to explain things he had felt at a gut level, but never put into words, while playing. Glen Albaugh, who taught sports psychology at Pacific, recalled him as a student "extraordinarily interested in the whole area of consciousness."

"I gave him a reading list and he went through it really fast," Albaugh said. The books ranged from Eastern philosophy to Abraham Maslow, a leader in humanistic psychology. Maslow broke from traditions of psychoanalysis and behaviorism by insisting that each person held great potential waiting to unfold. This optimism suited Carroll, who said, "All of a sudden, things started to make sense." Maslow also wrote of peak experiences, what he called "a single glimpse of heaven," which Carroll equated to an athlete's being "in the zone," like a cornerback who breaks toward the sideline because preparation and instinct tell him a pass is coming.

As a graduate assistant on Caddas' staff, Carroll worked first with receivers, then the secondary. "He was always upbeat, always trying to figure out some way to get an edge," Caddas said. "He was constantly studying the game. From the ideas he came up with, you knew he was looking not at one side but at both sides." The 22-year-old was taking what he learned in the classroom and applying it to the field. He soon discovered, however, that not everyone shared his enthusiasm.

Pacific struggled during his three seasons there, scratching to finish at .500, most often falling short. At one point, Carroll called a meeting with his defensive backs, who were having a particularly rough time. He asked them which coverages felt most comfortable and which techniques they wanted to practice. It was a departure from the traditional football hierarchy by which coaches made all the decisions and athletes simply followed orders. Carroll recalled that his guys left the meeting feeling rejuvenated, but when he recounted the discussion with another coach on the staff, the older man interrupted, "Wait just a damn minute, boy. Don't you ever ask them what they want. You tell them what they need."

Carroll said, "I was totally deflated."

It did not take long to get back on his feet. In 1977 he worked as a graduate assistant for Lou Holtz at Arkansas, where the Razorbacks went 11–1, including an upset victory over Oklahoma in the Orange

An Unconventional Approach

Bowl. Monte Kiffin, an assistant on that squad, said, "Pete was just a young pup. He would sit in the back of the room and he wouldn't say much. But when I asked him questions, he always knew the answer. I told Lou Holtz, 'We're not going to keep this guy long because he's special.'"

Carroll moved on to Iowa State, then Ohio State. In 1980, Kiffin took over at North Carolina State and hired him as defensive coordinator, where he remained for three seasons. By 1984, Carroll had jumped to the Buffalo Bills, beginning an NFL career that would stretch 16 years and make him famous, if not always for the right reasons.

It is difficult to say exactly when the NFL slapped a wunderkind label on Carroll, maybe around the mideighties when he worked under Bud Grant as a defensive backs coach for the Minnesota Vikings. Grant recognized a special instinct in his young assistant, explaining once that "some head coaches don't have the ability to stand in the middle of a practice field and know everything that is going on. . . . Pete has all that and more."

By the time the New York Jets made him defensive coordinator in 1990, Carroll had refined his style of dealing with players face-to-face. Sometimes that meant cracking the whip, sometimes it meant talking about girlfriends and movies. He was clearly part of a new breed that had diverged from the authoritarian mode, of which he said, "That can be a great way to teach, but it's not me. I get more out of you if I connect with you. Instead of knocking you down . . . I'm going to build you."

There was a 1991 game in which the Jets were backed up against their end zone, needing a goal-line stand to hold off the New England Patriots. During a timeout, the defense came to the sideline and, instead of screaming and fist-pounding, got a big smile from their coordinator. "Do you understand how exciting this is?" Carroll asked. "How great this is?" Pat Kirwan, a former Jets executive, recalled listening over headphones in the booth and thinking, "What the heck?" It was trademark Carroll, a curious blend of boyishness, athletic instinct, and Maslow's notion of peak experience. He was certain that if his players could relax and enjoy the moment, they would come through.

"The guys were actually cheering," Kirwan recalled. "And we stopped them."

Sometimes Carroll went too far. The next season, against the Miami Dolphins, television cameras caught him giving the choke sign when the opposing kicker, Pete Stoyanovich, missed an extra-point attempt. The Dolphins came back to win, and it took years for Carroll to live that one down. Still, when the Jets promoted him to head coach in 1994, just short of his 43rd birthday, he wasn't about to change. His assistants soon found themselves on a plane, traveling to the Washington ranch of motivational guru Lou Tice, whose clients ranged from corporate and military leaders to former Los Angeles Dodgers slugger Kirk Gibson. In sessions that lasted from morning until late in the evening, they discussed an array of leadership issues.

On the third night, about 9:00, Tice was trying to get a serious point across when Carroll started to laugh. "God, I was exhausted," Tice said. "He couldn't stop giggling." Tice asked him what was so funny.

"It's three days and we're still getting information," Carroll said. "I just love it."

Tice and his wife, Diane, flew to New York a few months later to attend the Jets' exhibition game against the New York Giants. They knew Carroll too well to expect that he would be nervous. "His mind is different," Tice said. "The pressure doesn't get to him." As the team bus headed for Giants Stadium, the coach sat beside Diane, chatting. "People look at that and say he's distracted," Tice said. "No, he just knows how to think effectively." A few hours later, his team came from behind to win.

When the Jets began the regular season with two victories— thanks in large part to a tough, opportunistic defense—the new leader was praised as forward-thinking. But when they hit a losing streak, his style left him vulnerable to detractors. It only got worse after a particularly harsh defeat against Miami, quarterback Dan Marino faking as if to spike the ball, then straightening up and lofting an eight-yard touchdown pass in the final seconds. By late December, the Jets were staggering to a 6–10 finish and the view of Carroll had shifted dramatically. He was criticized for blaring rock 'n' roll music in his office and erecting a basketball hoop beside the practice field. He was too soft, too easygoing, a trespasser in the House of Lombardi. Team owner Leon Hess soon fired him.

For the next two years, Carroll served as defensive coordinator for the San Francisco 49ers where, again, his squad ranked among the best in the league. His reputation recovered sufficiently that, in 1997, the New England Patriots offered him their head coaching spot. Friends tried to warn him away. They said it was a losing proposition, if only because the previous coach had been Bill Parcells, an old-school authoritarian beloved in the region. Carroll took the job anyway.

On paper, his stint in New England was a moderate success. The Patriots reached the playoffs two out of three seasons and never had a losing record. But coming off a Super Bowl appearance under Parcells, they slipped a little each year, going from 10–6 to 9–7 to 8–8. The media wrote suspiciously about Carroll riding a bicycle to practice, organizing bowling nights, and playing touch football with his players. The *Boston Herald* wrote about the popular perception of him as a "transferred surfer from the West Coast who can't handle the pressure of coaching in the East." There was also friction with management, especially when the team let free-agent running back Curtis Martin slip away to Parcells and the Jets. Friends said Carroll's hands were tied. Compounding these issues, the coach later conceded, "I made some big mistakes."

Terry Glenn, the troubled receiver, was a consistent problem. And the *Boston Globe* ran a damaging story about a player who did not finish a mandatory run in training camp. According to an unnamed source, Carroll summoned the player to practice the next morning and suggested that he spray water on himself to give the impression of sweat, then tell his teammates he had completed the run. Team officials denied the incident took place. Still, there were rumblings, hints of discord in the locker room. A former Patriot, running back Dave Meggett, told reporters that Carroll ultimately lost control of a team that could not handle that kind of "laid-back" environment.

Even with all these problems, the coach's supporters pointed out that his 27–21 record equated to the best winning percentage in Patriots history at the time, even better than Parcells'. It was not good enough for owner Robert Kraft. "A lot of things were going on that made it difficult for him to stay, some of which were out of his control," Kraft told reporters. The team fired Carroll in January 2000.

———

Not long after he took over at USC, sitting in his upstairs office with classic rock playing softly over the stereo, Carroll recalled meeting Rick Barry at a sports banquet several years earlier. He had approached the former NBA star to ask about that "46 percent lifetime shooter" quote. Barry brusquely denied saying it, snapping back, "I was a 48 percent lifetime shooter." Carroll cringed at the time, but, years later, the memory made him laugh.

"Isn't that great?" he asked.

An Unconventional Approach

It was the fierce competitor in Barry that amused him. Friends say Carroll is wired like that, always pushing, striving to improve, looking for ways to make the most of each situation. In pickup basketball games, he played such persistent defense that Walt Harris used to tell him, "When you die, your hands will still be moving." And when he chatted with a player about home life or going out on the weekend, it was more than small talk. He was trying to understand the kid, get inside his head, figure out how to inspire him. "That was one of the reasons I wanted to play for Pete," said Ronnie Lott, who was on Carroll's team in New York. "I just liked the way he communicated. That energy level, that passion."

Getting fired by the Patriots put a damper on the flame, if only for a while. "Did I feel beaten down?" Carroll asked. "No, I was pissed." In no mood to retreat to another NFL coordinator's job, he took a break from coaching.

It was the first time in almost three decades that his spring and summer were not consumed with preparing for the next season. Carl Smith, who had been an assistant on his staff at New England, said, "In this business, you just rush through, no time to think about what you did right and what you did wrong. I think, for Pete, that year was about having time to himself. To sort a lot of things out." Carroll did some media work and explored going into business. He thought about leaving football entirely, but the game was hard to shake. "I took a look at what retirement is and found out I didn't like it," he said.

Two things happened. First, he read a book by legendary UCLA basketball coach John Wooden, who wrote about what Carroll describes as "the power of knowing exactly what you want to get done." It was a seminal moment. Carroll thought about the type of coach he wanted to be, what felt natural to him. If anything, this persuaded him to refine his style, to make small adjustments, but not to change. Of the boundless energy and optimism, the desire to relate to his players, "That's who I am," he said. And if he truly believed in himself, wouldn't his players believe too?

At the same time, his son, Brennan, was playing tight end for the University of Pittsburgh, and Carroll spent Saturday afternoons watching the games. After all those years in professional football, a change of scenery appealed to him, and Smith recalled that Carroll was "getting psyched . . . pointing himself toward the college game." It wasn't the first time he had considered a switch. Back in 1997, when USC fired Robinson, the school approached Carroll about taking the job. Daryl Gross, the senior associate athletic director, said the offer was $1 million a year. Carroll confirmed there were discussions but said he could not recall an exact figure. Regardless, he was guiding the Patriots to the playoffs in his first season at New England and had no interest in leaving.

Three years later, when he heard that Paul Hackett was fired, Carroll decided to take a shot at the job. He and Gross said they could not remember who made contact first, but after a few conversations, a meeting was scheduled. The media were already talking about Dennis Erickson and Mike Bellotti, so Carroll wondered if Athletic Director Mike Garrett would give him a fair shot. No matter, his innate competitiveness kicked in to high gear. He studied the USC program, its strengths and weaknesses, honing a presentation. Then he got on a flight to Los Angeles, feeling excited.

"I needed to be ready," he said. "I had a huge interview opportunity and wanted to be sure I could nail that."

CHAPTER 5

"Turn the Switch On"

The new coach had been on campus about a month, and his players were still getting to know him. Carson Palmer, the quarterback, had spoken with Pete Carroll a few times and said that he seemed "real down to earth." But then Carroll made an unusual request. He asked the team to meet him at the Coliseum. In the dead of winter. In the middle of the night. Lenny Vandermade, an offensive lineman, thought, *This is something new.*

It was pitch dark outside as the Trojans gathered on the floor of the stadium, surrounded by all those rows of empty seats. A heavy rope lay across the turf, and Carroll divided his players, offense versus defense, for a tug of war. Memories of that night differ. Some players said that after the two sides struggled against each other, the coach had them all get on one end of the rope and pull together. Other players said that he had them stop and stand close together. Either way, Carroll gave an impassioned speech about what he called "the power of collective effort," and the message was simple: unless they worked together, the Trojans would get nowhere. "I don't know if everyone bought into it," tight end Alex Holmes said. "I did. I could see things were going to get better."

Shortly after the pep talk, USC began its off-season workouts.

The thrill of September, the crowds and marching bands, seemed very far away as young men dragged themselves out of bed early in the morning—sometimes in the dark—to run sprints on the track or lift weights. Though hardly glamorous, conditioning represented an essential part of Carroll's plan for turning the program around. He had inherited only a handful of athletes who could bench-press more than 400 pounds, only a few who could power-clean more than 300, and his linemen were carrying too much body fat. A new strength coach—Chris Carlisle from Tennessee—was hired to make the team stronger and lighter.

While players worked out in the basement, Carroll was upstairs in his office from morning until late at night. No time to read newspapers or listen to sports-talk radio, no interest in hearing any more negative reaction to his hiring. "I've kicked into full competitive mode," he said. "Turn the switch on and go at it." Calls poured in by the dozens, a blur of ringing telephones and voice messages, many of them starting with the same "Congratulations, Pete. And by the way . . ." It seemed as if every unemployed assistant in the nation wanted a few minutes of his time, knowing full well that he was assembling a staff. Foremost on the list was offensive coordinator. "It's a critical hire," Carroll said. "I've done tons of homework." Word soon leaked that he was going after Norm Chow.

For the better part of three decades, Chow had been integral to the offense at Brigham Young. A quiet man, words tinged by the pidgin accent of his native Hawaii, he ranked among the finest minds in college football, his wide-open passing attack producing one exceptional quarterback after another: Steve Young. Robbie Bosco. Ty Detmer, the Heisman Trophy winner. After the 1999 season, with no chance at BYU's head coaching job, Chow jumped to North Carolina State and promptly turned freshman Philip Rivers into a star.

Carroll had a pool of money from which to hire a staff but now went back to Mike Garrett to ask the athletic director for more. "I need this guy," he said. Daryl Gross, the senior associate athletic director, recalled, "Pete really marketed Norm to us. Maybe the pool of money increased. You know, x plus 50." North Carolina State was willing to bump Chow's already hefty salary to $180,000. Carroll came in with an offer of approximately $250,000, plus incentives, and some advantages that money could not buy.

Los Angeles was hundreds of miles closer to Utah, where Chow's family still lived while his youngest son finished high school. The coordinator could hop on a plane and be home for a visit in a little over an hour. As corny as it might have seemed, Chow also was intrigued by "the white horse that runs around the Coliseum" and all the other trappings that came with Trojan football. "It just sounded like a situation that would be fun, would be exciting," he said.

News of his hiring started a buzz around campus. Palmer could not help grinning at the thought of operating out of a spread offense, and receiver Kareem Kelly said, "It's going to be a complete turnaround. You can just feel the reaction and energy." But while Chow's arrival made headlines, another personnel move—less heralded—would prove every bit as important.

———

A tall wooden fence ran the perimeter of the USC practice field, a heavy metal gate keeping out the uninvited. However, those who wandered past on the sidewalk—students, faculty, fans—did not have to see inside to know about the man called "coach O." They could hear him.

Ed Orgeron was built like a cement truck, a wide load, with a voice to match. It started down deep in his barrel chest, rumbling, gathering momentum. Whenever he grew excited, which was not at all unusual when it came to football, the defensive line coach could rattle windows, if not the confidence of freshmen. "He's pretty loud," said Matt Grootegoed, a safety at the time. "At first, it's kind of, *What have I gotten myself into?*"

Conquest

After playing four years at out-of-the-way Northwestern State in his native Louisiana, Orgeron started coaching in the mideighties and soon worked his way onto Jimmy Johnson's staff at Miami. The Hurricanes were on a torrid streak, winning two national championships in three years, as Orgeron nurtured a succession of All-American linemen that included future NFL stars Cortez Kennedy, Russell Maryland, and Warren Sapp. He hit a rough patch, including a couple of arrests for bar fights, and took some time off to put his life in order before returning to football. In 1998, Paul Hackett brought him to USC.

His personality dominated the practice field, that roar and the way he scrambled around in drills, getting in his guys' faces. If he seemed harsh at first, the assistant ultimately proved as caring and funny as he was intense, and players such as Grootegoed came to love him. He also was extremely valuable to the program because he brought the same fierce attitude and rough-hewn Southern charm to the work of recruiting.

College programs live and die by their ability to keep the roster stocked with fresh talent. The courtship between recruiters and top-notch high school players can be delicate, a relationship forged on notes in the mail, telephone calls, and critical hours spent in the family living room. "You have to be relentless," Orgeron said. In his first few years at USC, the Trojans were anything but. They were still relying on reputation to attract the best prospects and, as a result, homegrown talent was slipping away to the likes of Washington, Texas, and Notre Dame. "What happened?" Carroll asked upon arriving. Orgeron was blunt, saying, "We haven't done a good job . . . just the whole philosophy of hard work, being thorough."

Carroll took an immediate liking to the guy, saying, "He was so fired up. I just felt like he might be special." Orgeron not only remained on the staff, he got a promotion to recruiting coordinator.

"Turn the Switch On"

The two men were a good match, both so energetic, constantly challenging each other. Their first task was to reestablish ties with local high school coaches who had not heard from USC in years, and they made a contest of it, seeing who could visit the most campuses each day. "We were just being stupid and really having fun," Carroll said. Next, they needed to reassure recruits who had made verbal commitments to Hackett and were wavering. Soon enough, Matt Leinart, the Parade All-American quarterback, was steered away from Oklahoma and back to the Trojans. After so many years in the pros, Carroll overcame a slight case of nerves—"I've got to work on my spiel," he said at one point—and developed a rhythm with Orgeron, traveling from home to home, wooing all those young men and their parents. Offensive lineman Sam Baker, who came along a few seasons later, tells a typical story.

Orgeron made first contact and, as Baker recalled, "He was such an awesome guy . . . he'll fire you up." Then it was Carroll's turn. With recruiters coming through one after another, Baker had arranged furniture in his living room so that he and his mother could sit across from visitors, almost as if conducting a formal interview. Carroll would have none of it. He barged into the house, pushing everything aside, and plopped down on the couch between the player and his mom. "A lot of coaches are so serious . . . you can't see yourself going to them with problems," Baker said. "Coach Carroll is one of those guys you can relate to."

But Carroll and Orgeron brought more than personality to the recruiting game—they also made a promise to young players. USC would not follow the traditional route of keeping freshmen on the bench. *If you're good enough*, they said, *you can play right away*. That first spring of 2001, this policy helped them beat out Notre Dame and Washington for defensive end Shaun Cody, a prep All-American whom Carroll referred to as "a cornerstone for our program." In all, the Trojans signed a 17-player class that drew high praise from recruiting experts. The program figured to need every last man.

———

The experience in New York back in 1994 had taught Carroll a lesson. When the Jets promoted him from defensive coordinator to head coach, he became more of an administrator, supervising from above, and lost that close contact with his team. "We lost our identity," former safety Ronnie Lott said. "Pete, as a coach, looks back at that moment and thinks, *God, I should have stayed more engaged.*" He would not make the same mistake at USC.

The start of spring practice found Carroll constantly moving around the field, looking crisp in khaki pants and a polo shirt, his body at a forward tilt. "My circling habits," he explained. The early part of each day was spent scrutinizing the offense, talking to linemen, advising receivers on their routes. "I like getting into it," he said. "There's always a teachable moment waiting for me." Next, his focus turned to defense. Carroll was so determined to be hands-on that he decided to serve as his own defensive coordinator, which meant working daily with everyone, from cornerbacks to tackles, teaching coverages and angles of pursuit. "He knows a lot," linebacker Aaron Graham said. "You try to listen to every detail." But this was about something more than fundamentals. Carroll was proving himself, motivating players the best way he knew how—face-to-face.

His efforts did not stop with the final horn. The new coach usually stayed after practice, grabbing someone for a game of catch, and that first spring it was often Kori Dickerson. The senior was switching from linebacker to tight end, so Carroll showed him hand positions for different types of catches, how to fall to his knees for low passes. A kind of folklore was building, stories that would one day swirl around the program, like the time Carroll stepped in at quarterback during a goal-line drill, throwing himself into the fray. Or the time he led his team to the Olympic diving pool next door, the first to climb the tower and jump off the high platform. "He brought his intensity and his love and his passion for the game," Palmer said later. "Everybody is fired up, jumping up and down on the sideline. Guys on the field are happy, flying around and slapping each other. That's coach Carroll."

The change from Hackett—a technical wizard who could seem aloof—was striking if only because players found they could approach Carroll at almost any time. "The coaches can be sitting in a meeting room, in the deepest discussion about the most important thing, but the second a player walks in the door, the discussion stops," Orgeron said. "The players know they can talk to us." Defensive lineman Lonnie Ford called it "a whole different vibe." Charlie Landrigan, the fullback, explained, "It's being able to go and talk to him . . . about everyday things, what's going on in school, what movies you've seen."

But Carroll wanted to be tough, too. Maybe, just maybe, a few of those critics from the New England days had worked their way under his skin, and now, as his friend Carl Smith said, "He tightened some things down." Never the type to grab face masks or scream, he sought to exert discipline in other ways. Malcolm Wooldridge, a defensive lineman, found himself crawling on hands and knees from one end of the field to the other, punishment for neglecting to get his ankles taped. Dickerson arrived at practice a few minutes late and spent the rest of the afternoon doing push-ups. "That let the team know he's strictly business," the tight end said. "If you break a rule, you have to pay."

It was a concentrated effort to establish, as quickly and fully as possible, a new culture within the program. This sort of thing goes on every time a new staff takes over. "So much work to do," Carroll said. Of course, conventional football matters also required his attention.

Conquest

Amid all the hoopla over Chow's hiring, Carroll had insisted that USC could win with defense. This amounted to heresy in the Pacific-10 Conference, where the games tended to be high-scoring. Carroll knew that he was taking an unusual approach and said, "I liked that it sounded different." Again, he had an ally in Orgeron, who had watched Jimmy Johnson build the Miami dynasty in much the same way. "Nobody in the Pac-10 played defense," the assistant said. "Pete was smart." It would not be an easy process. Key defensive players, such as linebackers Zeke Moreno and Markus Steele, had gone to the NFL, leaving holes to fill, and the line would need freshman Cody to make an immediate impact.

Considerably more talent returned on offense, starting with Palmer and tailback Sultan McCullough, who had rushed for 1,163 yards the previous season. The fast-if-inconsistent Kelly was back at receiver, along with a younger, promising Keary Colbert. The question was, could the linemen improve sufficiently to lead the way? Several of the new assistants privately marveled that once-mighty USC could be so thin along the front. Not much speed. No killer instinct. And could the offense handle a crash course in Chow's brand of magic? Multiple-receiver sets, lots of motion, plenty of shotgun. The very first scrimmage, the Trojans ran a reverse with a pass back to the quarterback. Kelly talked about staying up late to study the playbook—"It's been tough . . . lots of gimmicks"—and the players sometimes appeared confused, if not overwhelmed. Chow was intentionally bombarding them with information, promising that, "We'll pull back later."

To make things even tougher, the coaching staff had to devote a fair amount of time to remedial lessons. Namely, holding onto the ball. USC had finished the previous season with the second-to-worst turnover ratio in the nation. So, from day one, Carroll harped on taking care of the ball, and assistant Wayne Moses, newly arrived from Washington, tutored the running backs on proper cradling technique.

On the flip side of this emphasis, the defense was urged to force turnovers. "Every chance they get, they're slapping at it, pulling at it, jumping routes," Palmer said. "It's a little nerve-racking."

At night, watching film of each afternoon's practice, the coaches noticed gradual improvement. If only there were more time, more than a few weeks' worth of sessions. In the final scrimmage of the spring, the offense appeared out of sync and could not sustain a drive. McCullough fumbled, and Palmer threw three interceptions, reviving painful memories of seasons past.

"Sloppy," Palmer said. "Just a bad way to end."

———

The coaches came away from spring ball with a better idea of the challenge that lay ahead. There seemed to be enough talent to assemble a winning team, but the margin of error would be slim. So slim, in fact, they were counting on a guy who only a year earlier had been on his death bed.

Antuan Simmons had come to USC in 1997 as a defensive back pressed into action in the second game of the season. The kid from Sacramento responded with 11 tackles. "Didn't blink once," said Dennis Thurman, an assistant then. Although Simmons could be maddening at times, given to mental lapses, not always the hardest worker in practice, there was no questioning his raw physical talent.

Shifting from safety to cornerback as a sophomore, he started about half the games and, against Washington, intercepted two fourth-quarter passes, returning both for touchdowns. As a junior, he became a full-time starter and had a big game against Stanford, intercepting another two passes and recovering a fumble. Simmons also played on special teams, blocking a half-dozen kicks during his first three seasons, and was popular among teammates. "If I had a question about how to cover a guy or something I should be doing better, he was there to tell me," said Kris Richard, a fellow defensive back. "He was there to lean on."

His problems began with a nagging back injury during that junior season of 1999. The pain grew unbearable, requiring emergency surgery to relieve pressure on a nerve. It was during a follow-up examination that doctors noticed unusual blotches on the X-rays—a cluster of tumors had formed along his aorta and wrapped around his left kidney.

Simmons went right back into the operating room, this time for six hours, surgeons carefully removing the benign masses and reconstructing a major vein. He developed internal bleeding, which required yet another operation, and his short hospital stay stretched into weeks. "It became a nightmare," he said. The once-powerful athlete lost 35 pounds and traveled in and out of intensive care, breathing through a respirator as he battled further complications. His muscles atrophied to the point where he needed help to stand. Teammates and coaches stopped by to cheer him up, maybe talk some football, shaking their heads as they walked away. Hackett, still the coach, said, "If it's you or me . . . we're dead."

Watching a clock on the wall of his room, waiting for a time when things would get better, Simmons refused to give up hope. The turning point came in late June 2000 when doctors discovered the cause of his labored breathing: more than a liter of fluid had developed around his heart. Simmons was too weak and sedated to realize that he was going in for yet another procedure, but upon waking, he sensed that something had changed. His body started to grow stronger. Some two months after arriving at the hospital, he finally went home.

By August, Simmons was healthy enough to accompany the team to New Jersey and watch the opener against Penn State. After USC's victory that day, Paul Hackett handed him the game ball. It was an emotional moment, a symbol of his return, but the tough part was far from over. While the Trojans struggled through the season, Simmons had to put on pounds and coax his muscles back into shape. The experience changed him, he said, made him treasure school and family, made him appreciate the game he had occasionally taken for granted.

All the weight eventually returned, his legs recovering their spring, and in March 2001 the defensive back convinced coaches that he could return to the field. "We were stunned he was even out at spring practice," Carroll said. "He was hitting the heck out of people and making plays." Exactly what the Trojans needed.

———

It was an odd defensive call, a blitz that sent linebackers scurrying after the quarterback, and defensive tackle Bernard Riley—all 315 pounds of him—backpedaling like crazy into pass coverage. Not only did Riley intercept the ball 15 yards downfield, he turned and lumbered up the sideline, doing his best imitation of someone who could actually run. In the heat of a late August practice, his teammates did not know whether to cheer or fall down laughing.

"That's Pete Carroll and his defensive genius," associate head coach DeWayne Walker said. "You'll see some funny-looking stuff."

As with any sleight of hand, transforming the Trojans would require quickness. Through early summer, the players had been on the track beside Heritage Hall, working on their sprint technique. When training camp began, they were reminded of the new cardinal rule: no walking. Everything was swift and efficient, everyone hustling from one drill to the next. The staff kept track of "loafs"— instances when an athlete stopped short of the whistle—and violators were sentenced to crawling or push-ups. "Last year, this team as a whole was stagnant," said Holmes, the tight end. "We don't want to be like that anymore."

As practices grew more and more intense, Carroll found a way to turn the pressure up even higher. No one was guaranteed a starting spot, he announced. Each position was up for grabs each and every day. In this manner, the coach hoped to create a team that matched his own hyper-competitive personality, every bit as fiery and tireless. Midway through camp, a handful of lineman found themselves fighting over two open slots along the front five. Same thing at linebacker.

"That's what every practice is about, every drill, everything we do is some form of competition," Holmes said. "At first it was hard for a lot of guys. But once they started seeing results, once they knew it was making us better, they realized how important it was." Some even grew to like it. Cody explained, "If you come out here and walk around, it gets monotonous. When you practice live action, it's almost like being in a game."

The emphasis on speed and grit translated into a thoroughly reshuffled defense. Safeties Frank Strong and Matt Grootegoed were shifted forward to become undersized linebackers. Mike Pollard, who had played on the edges, was recast as a 225-pound middle linebacker. Though initially reluctant—"I was kind of mad"—he soon challenged Aaron Graham for the starting spot. In theory, at least, Carroll had fashioned a squad that was small and quick enough to swarm to the ball.

About the only thing that could not be accelerated was the learning curve for Palmer and the offense, still straining to acclimate to Chow's rapid-fire system. As days went by, the coordinator groused, "We're not as far as we'd like to be." It did not help when Malaefou MacKenzie, a versatile tailback expected to play in passing situations, was sidelined by a sore knee. Or when receiver Marcell Allmond got into trouble for fighting on campus and was suspended from school for the semester.

With the roster so thin, every loss hurt. Carroll waited for two of his best recruits, linebacker Marvin Simmons and defensive lineman Ray Tago, to qualify academically, but it never happened. As the season opener against San Jose State drew near, the coach tried not to dwell on the negative. Facing perhaps his last shot at running a team, he figured, "Either it was going to happen or it wasn't. I was just going to go for it."

CHAPTER 6

"We Don't Have to Lose Anymore"

T he team bus normally pulled around back of the Coliseum on game day, letting players off close to their locker room, but Pete Carroll had something else in mind for the 2001 season opener. He told the driver to stop in front of the stadium. From there, the Trojans walked across a plaza filled with alumni and fans, through an iron gate, and down the peristyle steps to the field. "Walking into the Coliseum is a very special experience," the new coach said. "I wanted them to see that."

A few of his guys admitted to feeling chills. "Kind of cool," quarterback Carson Palmer said of what would become a pregame ritual at USC. "It's good to get some tradition."

Not much was expected of the Trojans that fall. They were not nationally ranked, and only a small crowd—fewer than 46,000—showed up for their first game against San Jose State. If anything, fans were curious to get a look at Norm Chow's vaunted aerial attack. Instead, they got something more traditional. With the Spartans dropping extra defenders into pass coverage and Palmer vowing to be patient, tailback Sultan McCullough did most of the damage, breaking free on one run after another to give his team a 14–0 lead.

While the running game got off to a quick start, Carroll's streamlined defense showed it could attack the ball, keying on San Jose

State's main weapon on offense, tailback Deonce Whitaker. Safety Troy Polamalu played up close while linebackers Matt Grootegoed and Frank Strong—the converted defensive backs—used their speed to get into the backfield. Time and again, they hit the jitterbug Whitaker before he could get started. "Man," he kept telling them, "you guys swarm."

The Trojans, who had needed a late rally to defeat this team the previous season, cruised to a 21–10 victory. McCullough finished with 167 yards and all three touchdowns, giving Palmer a chance to ease into the new offense. There weren't a lot of penalties or turnovers, not like before. At the final gun, players celebrated the start of a new era by dumping Gatorade over Carroll's head and gathering in front of the band, waving victory signs as if they had won the Rose Bowl. It was left to Chow, the old hand, to sound a cautionary note, grumbling that the Trojans had yet to face a real test. They would not have to wait long.

The next week, 12th-ranked Kansas State came to town with a dangerous option offense, especially challenging for a West Coast team that rarely faced it. The Wildcats also figured to play strong against the run, bringing extra men into the box, leaving their talented defensive backs in single coverage. This presented some intriguing possibilities for Chow, a chance to hit the receivers with quick passes and let them try to break longer runs. At least, that was the plan.

"Big opponent," offensive tackle Eric Torres said. "You can see the excitement in people's eyes."

When Saturday came around, Kansas State raced to a 10–0 lead by running quarterback draws, the nimble Ell Roberson going for big gains. It was an arduous day for the USC defense. The Trojans would surrender a whopping 340 yards on the ground, a statistic that would later make Carroll shake his head. Still, his guys adjusted and eventually found ways to keep the Wildcats out of the end zone.

The offense was another story. As expected, Kansas State crowded the line against McCullough, who had been so effective the week before, and left its cornerbacks one on one. The problem was, Kareem Kelly and the rest of the receiving corps could not get open. If the Trojans were going to pull off an upset, Palmer had to find another way to move the ball. At a sturdy 6'5"—hardly as fast or elusive as Roberson—he nonetheless rumbled upfield on a 13-yard scramble to set up a short touchdown. A blocked extra point left the score at 10–6. Then, with five minutes remaining, Palmer got one more chance.

A 27-yard scramble pushed the ball across midfield. Next came a 12-yard pass to tight end Alex Holmes. The Trojans were close enough for a field-goal attempt, but that botched extra point had cost them—they would need a touchdown. Palmer slipped out of the pocket and took off running again. Two defenders quickly zeroed in. "When you're trying to get the first down, you're not going to get it by sliding," Palmer said. "The only way I was going to get it was by taking on those guys." A violent collision jarred the ball loose, and Kansas State recovered with 2:33 on the clock.

There was no Gatorade dumping, no celebrating in front of the band. In the quiet of the locker room, Carroll looked for a silver lining, noting that his team had come within four points of a nationally ranked opponent. "This is one of those games you've just got to keep fighting and scratching, and we did all that," he said. USC needed to remain optimistic—the next several weeks would include road games against Oregon, Washington, and Notre Dame.

Maybe the quietest player in that locker room after the Kansas State game had been Sultan McCullough. He was the forgotten man, carrying the ball only sporadically, gaining a paltry 40 yards. "Our whole plan was to pass the ball," he said. "We were trying to get the receivers and offense clicking." Although he wasn't complaining—at least not in so many words—it was obvious that he yearned for a larger role.

In a long line of USC tailbacks, McCullough had never quite fit the mold. Not as tough as Mike Garrett. Not as dazzling as O. J. Simpson or Charles White. Not an all-around back like Marcus Allen. He compensated with two very different qualities.

The first and most obvious was natural-born speed. The son of a man who had run track in college, he was built like a sprinter, lithe and finely muscled. In high school, McCullough ran the 100 meters in 10.41 seconds and twice rushed for 2,000 yards in football, making prep All-American teams in both sports.

Combined with this inherent talent was a motivation that bordered on vengeance. It had to do with his older brother, whom he idolized. They had played football in the yard as kids and, when asked, Sultan insisted that Saladin was the true star of the family, the one with all the moves. Back in the early nineties, Saladin ranked among the top high school backs in the nation and was set to attend USC until trouble over test scores left him ineligible. He drifted for a few years, playing at one junior college, then another. His college career ultimately included two decent seasons at Oregon, but his younger brother never got over what happened.

So when Sultan arrived at USC in 1998, he ran as if he had something to prove. "If I can do it, Saladin can do it twice as good," he said. "If I get 100 yards, it means he would have gained 200."

In his first game as a redshirt freshman, McCullough came off the bench to rush for 83 yards and a touchdown at Hawaii. Later that fall, he broke a 48-yard run against UCLA and had a good day against Louisiana Tech. The next season brought a chance to start and, staying injury-free after a history of hamstring problems, he gained 1,163 yards to finish among the top sophomores in the nation. As Oregon coach Mike Bellotti said, "The speed factor with Sultan McCullough is scary."

Entering his junior season, maybe the only thing that could slow him down was Chow's arrival. Conventional wisdom had the Trojans' shifting from "Tailback U." to something west of BYU, emphasizing ball control through the air. McCullough toed the company line, saying only that he wanted to fit somewhere in the new scheme. "If they throw the ball to me, if I'm a decoy, it doesn't matter," he said. Still, people within the program wondered how he might handle the change.

In training camp, it did not seem so bad. There were opportunities to run from the spread offense, those multiple-receiver formations stretching the defense, opening seams. When McCullough scored on a nifty dash during a preseason scrimmage, Carroll said, "I am hoping he can make a really big difference for us." And the season had started with such promise against San Jose State.

Then came Kansas State, and McCullough's disappointment was apparent. If nothing else, maybe the game showed that Palmer and the receivers had a ways to go in learning Chow's system. They were still struggling with quick adjustments at the line, the quarterback sorting through various options in a matter of seconds as the play developed. McCullough suggested that—for the time being, at least—he could take up the slack.

"We know the run is going to be a factor," he said. "We're going to shove it down their throats."

The third week of the season was supposed to be restful, a bye on the schedule, but the Trojans would not get much chance to regroup. Days after the Kansas State game, terrorists hijacked four jetliners over the East Coast, using them for suicide attacks on New York City and the Pentagon. Football seemed inconsequential after September 11, practices canceled as the nation grieved. It was a subdued group of players that eventually reconvened to prepare for the Pacific-10 Conference opener at Oregon.

Almost four years had passed since a visiting team last won at Autzen Stadium, where the all-too-cozy dimensions pushed 45,000 screaming fans right up against the sidelines. The Trojans were tense going in—expecting to be heckled all game—and this supercharged atmosphere exploded when, about 45 minutes before kickoff, the teams got into a brawl worthy of a bar room. It started with two players shoving each other, then escalated into wild punches and bodies flying across the artificial turf. Even the coaches were arguing at midfield. The game that followed was every bit as feisty.

The Trojans quickly fell behind, mostly because Palmer had three passes intercepted in a little over a quarter. In the second half, however, he showed a fighter's spirit, picking himself up off the floor, throwing touchdown passes to McCullough and Kelly. When kicker David Davis made his third field goal of the night, USC had come all the way back for a 22–21 lead, only 10 minutes from an upset victory over the seventh-ranked team in the nation. "You think the game is over," Palmer said. "You think you've got it won."

In the end, they needed one more first down to run out the clock. Carroll and Chow decided to play it safe, calling for two running plays. When they finally sent in a pass, Palmer threw the ball away instead of taking a sack. Oregon saved its final timeout and, getting the ball back with 56 seconds remaining, made the Trojans pay. Quarterback Joey Harrington, who had a history of last-second wins, completed five of six passes, driving his team into USC territory. With 12 seconds remaining, the Ducks kicked a 32-yard field goal to win, 24–22.

Bellotti had kind words for the losing team, a program he had rejected during a coaching search months earlier, saying USC was on the rise. His endorsement did not change that the Trojans had lost a game they dearly wanted, one that could have put them back on the map. Even worse, they now had two consecutive losses. The players insisted it wasn't like seasons past, when they had fallen into long slumps. Cornerback Kris Richard held his thumb and forefinger an inch apart and said they were "this close . . . a pinch away from being where we want to be." They remained upbeat through the next week of practices, even as Malaefou MacKenzie, the talented third-down back, blew out a knee. Then came a home game against Stanford that looked familiar for all the wrong reasons.

Turnovers and defensive breakdowns. Dumb penalties and no semblance of a running game. All of which made for a 21–0 halftime deficit. At least one thing could be said about the Trojans—they showed an admirable capacity to scramble back. Special teams helped with a long punt return and a blocked field goal that was run back for a touchdown. It would not be enough. As the clock wound down on a 21–16 loss, scattered boos echoed through the Coliseum. "It's frustrating," fullback Charlie Landrigan said. "It's all in the details."

The defeat left the Trojans at 1–3, their worst start in 40 years. Far from rebuilding, they appeared to be sliding backward. In the locker room, the assistants seemed dazed, one of them saying of his own players, "What team was that? I didn't even recognize them." Carroll glanced at the final statistics and mumbled something about all the mistakes, then stopped short. "You've probably heard that before." He lingered for an hour or so, until the rest of the team was gone, then spoke quietly with a few writers from the local newspapers.

For a moment, this was a different Pete Carroll, as if a dark cloud had passed over. He spoke a little unsteadily, asking about previous seasons. Why were his players falling into old habits? Why didn't they get it? Just as quickly, his trademark optimism returned, tinged with a bit of defiance. If only the team would listen to him, believe in him, he was certain that he could turn this thing around.

Conquest

It was becoming a familiar, if distressing, refrain around USC. Whenever the offense struggled, the front line came under renewed scrutiny, haunted by ghosts with names such as Ron Yary, Brad Budde, and Anthony Muñoz. The 2001 season was no different.

After that promising start against San Jose State, the Trojans had managed only 100 rushing yards against Kansas State. Then 40 at Oregon. Then 28 against Stanford. Their ground game ranked last in the Pacific-10, and opposing defenses were coming after Palmer without hesitation, sacking him 11 times already, also worst in the conference. Carroll said, "We're getting crushed up front."

The legacy for USC linemen was almost as storied as it was for tailbacks. Brice Taylor and Nate Barragar started things rolling in the twenties. After that came Johnny Baker and Tay Brown. Yary and Ron Mix. Budde and Roy Foster. Muñoz and Bruce Matthews. During the eighties, the team produced eight All-American linemen, one after another. Then came a shift.

"You haven't had the head coach like a John McKay or a John Robinson who believes the foundation for a program is the running game," said Artie Gigantino, a former USC assistant. "There's more of an emphasis on throwing the football, period. There's nothing wrong with that, it's just a different philosophy."

The nineties brought only one All-American—Tony Boselli—and the 2001 crop was once again falling short of expectations. "Maybe we need extra effort," said Torres, the sophomore tackle. "Maybe it's concentration." Whatever the reason, they looked slower than the defenses they faced each week. "When I look at the USC line, I don't see a lot of athleticism," another former assistant said. Some critics blamed recruiting—the Trojans had simply picked the wrong guys. Others echoed Gigantino's assessment, noting that the new USC system placed even greater emphasis on throwing. A rival Pacific-10 coach said, "I see a bunch of guys who are being taught to backpedal and pass-protect instead of knocking the . . . out of somebody."

To be fair, the line was still young, mostly underclassmen paired with one junior and senior. Like the skill players, they were still learning Chow's offense, their confusion evident on a draw play against Stanford. The defensive front had shifted, putting a Stanford rusher in a spot where he wasn't expected to be. Instead of adjusting, the USC linemen went ahead with their pre-assigned duties, leaving the opponent unblocked and free to waltz into the backfield.

"We work on it in practice," sophomore center Lenny Vandermade said. "We're just not executing."

An increasingly battered Palmer refused to point fingers, insisting that the guys up front were working hard in practice and in the weight room. McCullough, for all his struggles, suggested that he could put the running game back on track with a few more broken tackles. The linemen themselves could only remain patient and remember the advice Budde had given them when he visited before the season.

"He told us that when the going gets tough, we should stay together," Vandermade said. "No matter what happens, stay together."

It started with a shoving match in practice, Kareem Kelly taking on defensive lineman Bernard Riley, who outweighed him by more than 100 pounds. The word spread quickly, one guy telling another and so on. When the final horn sounded that afternoon, as the coaches headed inside, the players gathered in a far corner of Howard Jones Field.

The seniors did most of the talking. Richard, the cornerback, pleaded with his teammates not to let the season slip away. Landrigan, the fullback, talked about the importance of winning their next game. Kelly was adamant.

"Things have got to change," the receiver said. "We all need to show a little more fire."

In the days since the Stanford loss, the coaches had reached some conclusions, too. Carroll looked at game film and saw far too many blown assignments, players out of position and confused. "I'm disappointed I didn't catch this sooner," he said. Only a few wrinkles were added to the game plan that week as the offensive line was given streamlined blocking schemes, and tailbacks worked at picking up blitzes. On defense, linebackers and the secondary needed to be clearer about their responsibilities. Eleventh-ranked Washington came next on the schedule, and USC could not afford to make so many mistakes.

On a blustery afternoon beside Lake Washington, the Trojans went back to basics, running early and often. The much-criticized line held its own as McCullough pounded out the yards. That allowed Palmer to be more choosy in the passing game, finding his tight end for short gains, calmly beating a linebacker blitz with a 21-yard touchdown throw to Landrigan. For the first time in a month, the Trojans reached halftime with a lead.

"We came out a different team," Palmer said. "I thought we played good across the board."

The momentum began to shift, however, in the third quarter. The Huskies seemed to gain confidence as reserve quarterback Taylor Barton came off the bench to connect on a pair of touchdown passes. Kelly let a beautifully thrown ball bounce off his hands at midfield and had to make up for it, sneaking behind the secondary for a 58-yard touchdown catch, just to get the score back to 24–24. Less than four minutes remained when Washington got the ball back. Barton stepped into the huddle, looked at his linemen and said, "Hey, fellas, this is on you. We have got to run the ball and get some first downs." It was Oregon all over again, another last-minute drive. Even the distance of the game-winning kick was the same, 32 yards—this one good for a 27–24 victory.

For all the improvement the Trojans had shown, they now had a four-game losing streak and were officially in a tailspin. The next week brought some respite—Palmer throwing for three touchdowns in a victory over lowly Arizona State—but even that game had its share of bad news. McCullough strained an abdominal muscle in the first quarter, leaving the backfield so thin that fullback Sunny Byrd had to step in at tailback. Things wouldn't get any easier against the next opponent, Notre Dame.

If there was one thing Carroll had been told from the outset, it was the importance of the Notre Dame and UCLA games. Athletic Director Mike Garrett had talked about it. Alumni and fans had communicated variations on a similar theme: *You had better beat our rivals.* So the Trojans went into South Bend and promptly blew the game with two critical gaffes.

They were holding another first-half lead, the Irish showing almost no signs of life, when the coaches inexplicably gave punter Mike MacGillivray the option of running a fake deep in his own territory. The field looked wide open to MacGillivray—right until cornerback Shane Walton came flying in to tackle him short of a first down. Notre Dame needed only four plays to score, closing the gap to 13–10.

The second breakdown came after halftime. With first-and-goal at the 1-yard line, the offense failed to score on three consecutive running plays. "I don't know," guard Zach Wilson said. "It seemed like a couple of missed blocks." Carroll settled for a field goal, explaining, "We figured it would be better to get something." A revitalized Notre Dame, led by quarterback Carlyle Holiday and tailback Julius Jones, scored on three of its next six possessions to pull away for a 27–16 victory. "This was a game I was hoping would jump-start us," Carroll said. "It could have been significant in a lot of ways."

The Trojans returned to Los Angeles with a 2–5 record and a dramatically different outlook on their season. The chances of winning four straight games and earning a bowl invitation seemed remote, as everyone hunkered down, preparing themselves for the long haul. "USC loves to win, but USC has to understand there are steps to take," Polamalu said. "There are building blocks to winning." Even Carroll injected a bit of "wait until next year" into his weekly news conference: "You might think this is going to drive me into the dirt, and I'm not going to be able to bounce back. But being the optimist, the eternal optimist, I keep looking for things that can help us down the road."

Fans would not be as patient. They now had evidence with which to condemn Carroll's hiring, and there was talk of benching Palmer, getting an early start on the next golden boy, freshman Matt Leinart. Booing at home games figured to grow louder as alumni saw the same old thing happening. Another losing season, another year removed from greatness.

———

As his team struggled, Carroll kept talking about getting the players to believe. He was referring to a culture of defeat, a group of young men who had grown accustomed to coming up short. Changing that would require more than Xs and Os. He needed them to battle through their doubts, and he was finding an unlikely ally in Mike Pollard.

The middle linebacker had a history of fighting back from adversity. The bad luck started in 1995 when, as a highly touted junior at Long Beach Poly, Pollard hurt his knee. Young and afraid the surgeon would make a mistake, he insisted upon having an epidural so he could stay awake and watch the procedure.

The injury healed in time for him to play as a senior and attract interest from recruiters, but then his test scores came back too low.

That meant a semester of hitting the books at a local junior college to qualify. And there was another season of waiting when he reached USC in 1998, playing behind All-American linebacker Chris Claiborne. Finally, with a shot at winning a spot in the starting lineup for the 1999 season, Pollard tore ligaments in the other knee. He recalled thinking, *It's over.*

In need of motivation—the will to come back one more time—he looked first to his father. Henry Pollard had worked for decades as a welder before the shipyards closed down, leaving him too young to retire, too old to get hired elsewhere. He started a business selling peanuts to support his family. "Talk about hard times," he said, laughing. "But you can't give up." His son adopted the same attitude, taking further inspiration from old films of Muñoz, the USC offensive lineman who had five knee operations and still became one of the greatest players at his position in pro football history.

"If he had five surgeries on his knees and could do that," Pollard said, "I knew I could do it with just two."

The road back began with decidedly unglamorous duty on the kickoff squad in 2000. He took his frustration out on opposing returners, delivering a series of highlight-reel hits. "I knew I could play if someone gave me a chance," he said.

The opportunity arose when Carroll arrived in 2001. The new coach looked at videotape of Pollard's special teams work and penciled him in at outside linebacker. Then, in an ironic twist, Long Beach Poly recruit Marvin Simmons failed to qualify academically—just like Pollard years before—leaving the Trojans thin in the middle. Despite his initial reluctance to switch, Pollard won the job by the end of training camp. "He just kept answering the bell," said DeWayne Walker, the associate head coach. "It's nice to see him out there playing like he is."

Using his quickness and hands to fend off blockers, Pollard led the team with 11 tackles against Oregon and Notre Dame. Linebacker coach Nick Holt explained, "He's never going to be the biggest guy or the fastest guy on the field, but he's working his butt off and making a lot of plays."

Before each game, Pollard gave a prayer of thanks and made a point of listening to his cleats clack down the tunnel that led onto the field. He looked up at all the people in the Coliseum. "All the stuff I went through," he said. "I didn't think this day would ever come." He was the embodiment of what Carroll needed to revive the Trojans.

———

Something inside Kris Richard told him the ball was coming his way. Call it instinct. Or experience. Maybe even karma.

The Trojans were playing at Arizona in late October, and the senior cornerback had given up an embarrassing touchdown earlier in the game, but this was no time for dwelling on failures. With two minutes remaining and the score tied, he saw his receiver cut toward the sideline. "Something just triggered," he said.

USC had traveled to Tucson in a precarious state, bordering on the malaise that can befall a program staring at its third consecutive subpar season, all the seniors watching their last chance at a Rose Bowl melt away. "I can't worry about that," defensive end Lonnie Ford said. "If I go in the tank, it'll be a chain reaction." Carroll described the situation as "difficult because all the goals we should be shooting for are not there for us right now." Which made it all the more startling when the team stormed to a 31–13 lead over Arizona by halftime. The defense blitzed incessantly, with Pollard harassing the Wildcats' quarterback and tipping a pass that was intercepted. "They stormed the fort," Arizona coach John Mackovic said. Palmer threw two touchdown passes and Byrd, the makeshift tailback, scored from a yard out.

Then the game reverted to a more familiar pattern: USC's offense misfired, the opponent scored in bunches. Richard let an interception slip away, and the ball landed in the receiver's arms for yet another touchdown. With 7:05 remaining, the Wildcats tied the score, 34–34, and USC appeared bound for another fourth-quarter loss.

Until Richard trusted his instincts.

It was a moment straight out of Carroll's theory of performance, that curious blend of sweat and confidence and peak experience. When the Arizona receiver curled toward the sideline, Richard jumped on the short route and intercepted the pass, sprinting 58 yards to the end zone. The touchdown gave his team a 41–34 win.

"Karma," he said. "I guess when you keep battling, good fortune will come."

On paper, the victory did nothing more than to improve the Trojans' record to 3–5. On paper, the chances of them running the table still seemed unlikely. Yet, in the locker room afterward, Carroll sensed that something essential had occurred, as if a spell had been broken. *Finally,* he thought, *my guys realize they can make the plays and get the breaks they need to win.*

This was what he told them: "We don't have to lose anymore."

CHAPTER 7

The Innovator

Eight months earlier, Carson Palmer hesitated a bit as he walked upstairs to the USC football offices. It was the spring of 2001, long before the start of the season, and the normally cool headed quarterback was nervous. He was going to meet his new boss.

Norm Chow had just arrived in Los Angeles but already carried a very Southern California label: passing-game guru. This was, after all, the offensive coordinator who had designed some of college football's most dynamic aerial offenses and had nurtured quarterbacks such as Steve Young and Ty Detmer. Now, he summoned Palmer inside his small, sparsely decorated office—a simple desk and chairs, a window overlooking some trees outside—and politely told him to sit down. They proceeded to talk about family. About classes. Anything but football.

The next few times they met, it was the same thing. "I just wanted him to feel comfortable," Chow said. "I wanted him to be able to speak his mind."

There would be time for Xs and Os later, time for discussions about the high-powered, quick-strike attack that Chow planned to install. First, the bespectacled 54-year-old coordinator with graying hair and a doctorate in educational psychology needed to connect with the 21-year-old junior. He needed to develop trust.

Their relationship was an absolute necessity, central to any hopes the Trojans had of rebuilding the program. Pete Carroll had known as much when he spent all that money to hire Chow, and he had given Palmer explicit instructions for the off-season. "It is Carson's job to catch up and follow coach Chow around," he said. So the informal chats between coordinator and quarterback eventually led to film-room sessions. Then to the practice field. As Chow and Palmer got to know each other over several months, Palmer told his father, "This guy is really cool."

Palmer was not referring to Chow's play-calling. He was describing the man's general conduct, his calm and unfailingly humble demeanor. He noticed how Chow's telephone constantly rang with calls from friends around the country. He noticed the manner in which Chow treated others. "He respects the lunch lady and the people who clean up the cafeteria," Palmer said. "If you put all the football stuff aside, he's a great person."

The quarterback was taking Carroll's words to heart, saying, "I need to learn to walk in his footsteps."

———

"When are you going to find a real job?"

Throughout Chow's football career, his mother, Thelma, would ask that question. It was a running joke. No one, not even Chow, had envisioned that the boy from Honolulu would become a coach, let alone so respected. "Not in my wildest dreams," he said. The game was not in his genes.

His father, Warren, was the son of Chinese immigrants. Lacking money for college, he had taken a job with the federal government at age 18. "A stock-boy kind of thing," Chow said. By the time Warren retired, he was a high-ranking customs official whose career might have advanced even further had he not repeatedly declined posts in locales ranging from Asia to San Francisco. "He didn't think that was the way to raise a family," Chow said. "I never forgot that." Thelma, a native of Hawaii, taught nursery school and doted over three sons: Leonard, Michael, and Norman, the youngest, born on May 3, 1946. "We were a close-knit family," Chow said. "Everyone was treated with respect."

At Punahou High in Honolulu, Chow played football for the first time. His coach, Charley Ane, had been a tackle at USC in the early fifties and later became one of the first Polynesians in the NFL, spending seven seasons with the Detroit Lions. Under Ane's tutelage, Chow developed into a smart, solid lineman. "We moved him around a lot because of his skills," Ane said. "He was never the center of attention, the spotlight was never sitting on top of him, and he never wanted to do anything that put himself in that position."

College football recruiters rarely ventured to the islands in the midsixties, but BYU and Utah caught wind of the mobile lineman— now standing 6'1", 220 pounds—and offered him scholarships. He chose Utah partly because other Hawaiians picked BYU. "Why do what everyone else was doing?" he asked. Besides, the Salt Lake City campus was closer to Boise, Idaho, where his brother Leonard had attended school and was living then. Adjusting to the mainland would not be easy. Chow had never been away from the islands, never seen snow, and recalls being "scared to death." It took football to pull him out of his shell and, more to the point, out of his dorm room. He played along the defensive front for two seasons, then requested a switch to the other side of the line. Utah coach Mike Giddings, a former USC assistant, said, "OK, you come to camp at 230 pounds and we'll make sure you play offense."

The day before practice started that season, a young running back from San Francisco visited campus. "If we get this guy, we're going to be good," Giddings said, assigning Chow and several teammates to show him around. The recruit's name? O. J. Simpson. According to Giddings, Simpson committed to Utah that day, signing a letter of intent. But when he returned home, USC's tenacious assistant,

Marv Goux, persuaded him to enroll in junior college for one more year before joining the Trojans and, as Chow puts it, "the rest is history."

Without Simpson in the backfield, the Utes finished 5–5 in 1966. Chow fared significantly better. He felt at home playing offensive guard, holding his own against future NFL star Curley Culp in a game against Arizona State. The shy junior also hit his stride off the field, dating a young woman named Diane Carter, who he had met in class. The next fall, he earned all-conference honors and was an honorable mention All-American, leading to a tryout with the Saskatchewan Roughriders of the Canadian Football League.

Knocked out of the game by a knee injury, he returned to Utah to marry Diane and earn a master's degree in physical education and a teaching certificate in special education. The couple then moved to Hawaii to teach at Waialua High, where Chow also took over the school's football team. "I was the youngest coach in Hawaiian football—and my teams looked like that," he recalled in typical, self-deprecating manner.

When Diane's father fell ill in 1973, they took a leave of absence and returned to Utah. Chow began a doctoral program at Brigham Young, if only because he did not want to get all his degrees from the same university. It would prove a fortunate choice. Needing money to pay bills, he wrote a letter to BYU coach LaVell Edwards.

"I asked if I could be a graduate assistant," he said.

———

BYU was not considered a preeminent passing team in the early seventies. In fact, in 1972, the Cougars featured the nation's leading rusher in Pete Van Valkenburg. Chow joined the staff the next fall, serving two years as a graduate assistant before Edwards hired him as recruiting coordinator and wide receivers coach. He shared an office with Doug Scovil, the offensive coordinator, who was in the process of transforming the program into a quarterback factory.

The colleagues spent long hours talking football. As Scovil shared his thoughts on the passing game, Chow listened attentively, taking detailed notes, offering ideas and suggestions when asked. He marveled at the way Scovil could make quarterbacks such as Gifford Nielsen, Marc Wilson, and Jim McMahon "feel like absolute geniuses." Through the latter part of the seventies, there was more to absorb from Scovil's successors, Wally English and then Ted Tollner. Finally, when Tollner left to become the offensive coordinator at USC in 1982, Edwards turned the play-calling over to Chow, who took all that he had learned from his mentors and added his own innovations to the playbook.

That first season, Steve Young threw for 3,100 yards. The next year was even better. With Chow directing the attack from his chosen perch in the press box and a more-experienced Young at the controls, the Cougars led the nation in passing and total offense, earning a trip to face Missouri in the Holiday Bowl. In that game, BYU trailed by three points with less than 30 seconds remaining and had a first down at Missouri's 14-yard line. Chow, forsaking convention, called for a trick play. Young handed off to the halfback, who faked a sweep, then threw back across the field to the quarterback. The pass barely cleared the outstretched hands of a Missouri defender before Young grabbed it and scurried into the end zone for a game-winning touchdown. "Instantaneously, I became this so-called great play-caller," Chow recalled, laughing. "I got saved by two inches! All of sudden we're innovative and creative, the whole nine yards because of those two inches. That just goes to show you how crazy this business is."

Things got even crazier in 1984 when Robbie Bosco led the team to an undefeated record and the national championship. The program was on a roll that would last 10 more years. All of those seasons ended with an invitation to a bowl game, and all but one ended with a winning record. In 1990, they defeated No. 1 Miami, and Detmer won the Heisman.

Along the way, there were overtures from larger programs, which Chow always rejected. By that time, he had three sons and a daughter and, like his father before him, was forging a career in a normally itinerant profession without moving his family once. "It was fun," he said. "We beat some big teams and I still had a family life. I still went home every night and helped the kids with homework." But the fun began to wane in the midnineties. The Cougars went on a roller-coaster ride, invited to a bowl game one year, staying home the next. "All of a sudden it hits you," Chow said. "Nothing lasts forever."

When things went wrong, it was the coordinator—not the coach—who took the heat from fans and media. "I was the butt of it all because LaVell was an icon," he said. In 1998 and 1999, the Cougars saw winning seasons end with bowl losses. Although Chow had been led to believe the head coaching job would be his eventually—whenever Edwards retired—it did not work out that way. The staff learned that none of them would have a shot at the position. Years later, Chow publicly claimed to harbor "no bitter or tough feelings." Privately, he told of a university administrator who used a racial slur to describe Chinese laborers while he was in the room. "It's over. History," Chow said. "But don't think I don't remember."

In early 2000, for the first time in his career, he seriously considered a move. "I wasn't going to sit there and in another year be told to coach racquetball." That January, while at an annual football coaches convention, he got a call from Chuck Amato. The one-time Florida State assistant head coach had just taken over at North Carolina State and was in the market for someone to run his offense. Amato assumed that Chow was still intent on remaining at BYU; he was calling to ask about someone else.

The Innovator

A few moments of silence ensued before Chow responded. He said the coach in question was OK. Then he asked, "What about me?"

———

Late January brought a ferocious winter storm to North Carolina—the worst in more than a century, almost two feet of snow falling on Raleigh—just in time for Chow to arrive. Two weeks had passed since his initial conversation with Amato, and he was in town for an interview. Even if the weather weren't a bad omen, there were other reasons for the native Hawaiian to think twice about picking up stakes and moving east.

A change would mean living apart from his wife and youngest son, who was attending school in Provo. After so many years working with players he had personally recruited, Chow would have to reshape someone else's athletes, a squad that was coming off a 6–6 season. "You got down there, looked around at what was coming back, and got really nervous," he said of the returning quarterbacks. But his apprehensions soon faded.

Amato was in the process of spending seven figures to assemble what became known as college football's first "million-dollar staff." He nearly doubled Chow's salary, to $165,000, and considered it money well spent, telling reporters, "It was a great steal for us to get a man of his reputation." For Chow, now among the highest-paid assistants in the country, the idea of calling plays for the Wolfpack seemed even more attractive when spring practice began and he got a look at a certain freshman.

Philip Rivers was the son of a high school coach and Alabama's state player of the year. He had graduated early to enroll at North Carolina State with hopes of competing for the starting job. His throwing motion was not exactly pretty, but the 18-year-old possessed just about everything else Chow looked for in a quarterback. At 6'5" and 236 pounds, he was big, strong, and, most importantly, extremely football-smart.

"I knew on the first day of spring practice Rivers was going to be the quarterback," Chow said. "I told Chuck, 'You might as well make the move.'"

Never before had Chow headed into a season relying on someone with so little experience. He was accustomed to playing guys who had spent two or more years with him on the practice field and in the film room, diligently learning his system. He wondered how Rivers would respond to game-day pressure and remained so unsure about that unorthodox throwing style that he called Seattle Seahawk coach Mike Holmgren, a former BYU assistant, to discuss mechanics. Lost in all of this was another consideration: the new coordinator was under pressure, too. At the first home game, T-shirts and banners throughout Carter-Finley Stadium announced: "It's Chow Time on the Chuck Wagon."

There was no need to fret. Rivers debuted by passing for 397 yards in a double-overtime victory over Arkansas State. A week later, he threw for more than 400 yards and beat Indiana with a last-minute, 47-yard touchdown pass. Not only did the Wolfpack finish the regular season at 7–4, averaging 31 points a game, but Rivers was named freshman of the year in the Atlantic Coast Conference.

As the team prepared to face Minnesota in the Micronpc.com Bowl, Chow's telephone rang. "Hey," said the upbeat voice on the other end of the line. "This is Pete Carroll."

———

Midway through the second quarter, Chow began to worry. North Carolina State was losing to Minnesota by more than three touchdowns. The offense looked horrible. Worse still, the game was on national television and Carroll was sure to be watching.

In fall 2000, coach Paul Hackett feels the pressure to break a string of mediocre seasons at USC. *Vince Compagnone/*Los Angeles Times.

Sultan McCullough, among the fastest Trojans tailbacks ever, stretches for a pass against California. *Kirk McKoy/*Los Angeles Times.

Linebacker Zeke Moreno is a bright spot on a team that finishes 5–7 in 2000.
Vince Compagnone/Los Angeles Times.

Pete Carroll and athletic director Mike Garrett at a December 2000 news conference announcing Carroll's hiring. *Gina Ferazzi*/Los Angeles Times.

Quarterback Carson Palmer spends the off-season getting to know his new offensive coordinator, Norm Chow. *Vince Compagnone*/Los Angeles Times.

Carroll celebrates a victory over UCLA in the locker room. The win earns USC a trip to the 2001 Las Vegas Bowl. *Lori Shepler*/Los Angeles Times.

Linebacker Matt Grootegoed (No. 6) and defensive end Omar Nazel smother Auburn running back Ronnie Brown in the 2002 season opener. *Lori Shepler/*Los Angeles Times.

After struggling early in his career, Palmer shines as a senior, guiding the Trojans to a 52–21 victory over UCLA in 2002. *Anacleto Rapping*/Los Angeles Times.

Palmer and Carroll after a win over Notre Dame, a performance that earned the quarterback the 2002 Heisman Trophy. *Richard Hartog*/Los Angeles Times.

Justin Fargas scores on a 50-yard touchdown run to help defeat Iowa at the 2003 Orange Bowl. *Wally Skalij*/Los Angeles Times.

Mike Williams' touchdown pass to Matt Leinart provides a signature moment in the 28–14 win over Michigan at the 2004 Rose Bowl. *Wally Skalij*/Los Angeles Times.

LenDale White finds room to run in USC's rout of Oklahoma in the 2005 Orange Bowl, prompting Carroll to hoist the national championship trophy. *Photos courtesy of Kirby Lee/The Sporting Image.*

The Innovator

At the time of their informal chat, Carroll had not yet been hired by USC. He got the job shortly thereafter and immediately asked Amato for permission to speak to Chow after the bowl season. But with the Wolfpack playing so badly, Chow was thinking, *Man, he's watching this game. He's not going to call me back.*

Then Rivers connected with his tight end for a short touchdown before halftime, just enough to give his team a little momentum. The quarterback got hot in the second half, on his way to 310 yards passing and another touchdown, leading North Carolina State to a 38–30 comeback victory. Rivers was named most valuable player of the game and, soon after, Carroll was on the line with Chow.

It wasn't just the marching band and the white horse that appealed to the coordinator. It wasn't just the proximity to Utah. On a more visceral level, he liked the idea of getting involved with a storied program that had hit tough times. "You knew it wasn't doing as well as it should have been," he said. "The challenge was there." And so was the money.

During all those seasons at BYU, Chow had watched head coaches' salaries shoot past $1 million a year while coordinators and assistants lagged far behind. His contract at North Carolina State had been generous, upping the ante for assistants across the country, and now the Wolfpack wanted to give him even more, a contract extension with a raise to about $180,000 a year. But USC was willing to put him near the very top of his profession, offering approximately $250,000. Calling his time in Raleigh "the most fun in coaching that I had ever had," Chow nevertheless walked away.

Not that the money changed him. Greeted with fanfare upon his arrival in Southern California, he responded with a characteristic shrug. When the media praised him as a genius, he scoffed that there was "nothing unique about this offense that hasn't been stolen from somewhere else." When fans expected miracles, he groused that his squad was not progressing nearly as fast as he would have liked. But for all his nonchalance, Chow was well aware of the stakes.

"The only reason we're here is because the other guys couldn't get it done," he said. "If we don't get it done, someone else will be sitting here."

The coordinator agonized through the first seven games of the 2001 season as Palmer, the young man he had worked so hard to cultivate, obviously struggled with the new offense. A dramatic victory over Arizona had given the Trojans reason to hope, but there was still so much left to be done.

CHAPTER 8

Knowing Where to Go

The play called for Carson Palmer to roll left and look for the tight end on a crossing pattern. But with his team only four yards from the end zone—four yards from beating Oregon State in overtime—the USC quarterback had another idea.

Faking a handoff, he turned to find a defensive back bearing down from the corner. No matter. Palmer was big enough to bull his way past the smaller man and keep moving. Looking ahead, he now focused on the end zone, not a doubt in his mind that he was keeping the ball. "I just remember seeing that pylon at the goal line," he said. "I just wanted to make sure I hit it."

The Trojans were back home at the Coliseum, riding the high of an emotional victory over Arizona the previous week but also teetering, knowing one more defeat would mean a losing record for the 2001 season. Their game against Oregon State had not been pretty, a sluggish affair in which neither offense had found much of a rhythm. Twice in the final minutes of regulation, with the score tied, the Beavers drove within comfortable field-goal range. Twice, all-conference kicker Ryan Cesca missed. At the start of overtime, Cesca finally put one through the uprights from 29 yards out. The score was 13–10, and USC had one last chance.

On the sideline, the coaching staff screamed at the offensive line. "We'd let the defense down so many times," center Lenny Vandermade said. "We couldn't squander another opportunity." They went out and blocked well enough for Sunny Byrd, the converted tail-back, to pound out a first down. Then came Palmer's turn. "Being the quarterback, you want the ball in your hands," he said. "You're expected to win the game." A nine-yard pass to tight end Alex Holmes moved USC inside the 5-yard line. One play later, the coaches called for a pass. Did it cross Palmer's mind that he had fumbled on a game-ending drive against Kansas State only two months earlier? If so, the memory did not stop him.

Tucking the ball away, charging toward that orange pylon at the front corner of the end zone, he found himself in a race with a fast-approaching linebacker. Just four more yards. Palmer dived at the last instant, getting slammed to the turf as he crossed the goal line.

His teammates came rushing off the bench, piling on him, as the scoreboard registered a 16–13 victory. Barely a month removed from a four-game losing streak, the Trojans had turned themselves around. They were 4–5 and not afraid to peek into the future with two games remaining against California and UCLA, and a chance at a winning record after everyone had written them off. "We want to get to UCLA week where we're still alive for a bowl game," defensive lineman Ryan Nielsen said. "Anything can happen in the UCLA game."

Cal wasn't likely to stand in the way. The Golden Bears were winless, and their coach, Tom Holmoe, had already announced that he would resign after the season. On a drizzly afternoon in Berkeley, USC made quick work of them. The Trojans scored on the ground and through the air, on a fake field-goal attempt and an interception return, all of it adding up to a 55–14 rout. "We needed to score points to get some confidence," Palmer said. "We just got that attitude and shoved the ball down their throats." It was exactly as Carroll had predicted back at Arizona when he announced, "We don't have to lose anymore." His guys were playing confident and aggressive, expecting good things to happen, expecting the other team to get the bad breaks. All they needed was one more victory.

Earlier in the season, no one would have given them a chance of beating UCLA, not when their cross-town rival was 6–0 and ranked among the top teams in the nation. But the Bruins began to fall apart after tailback DeShaun Foster was declared ineligible for borrowing a car—an "extra benefit" in NCAA terms—from an actor-director named Eric Laneuville. Then came news that quarterback Cory Paus had been convicted of drunk driving before the season and kept it a secret. The Bruins lost three consecutive games, slipping to No. 20 in the rankings. By the time they met USC in a packed Coliseum in mid-November, these were programs headed in opposite directions.

On the game's opening possession, the Trojans drove quickly downfield, Palmer throwing a four-yard touchdown pass to receiver Keary Colbert, who was on the field despite two badly sprained ankles. Then the defense came out with a dizzying array of blitzes and stunts and, at one point, a zone drop that had defensive end Omar Nazel covering a UCLA split end. "We called everything on the sheet about three times," Carroll said. As the first quarter ended, Paus tried a pass to the left flat but the ball glanced off receiver Brian Poli-Dixon and hit defensive back Antuan Simmons on the thigh. In a moment that seemed frozen, almost like a special effect in the movies, Simmons trapped the ball against his body with one hand, slid it behind him and back up through his legs. While everyone on the field stood watching, the senior—who had nearly died from abdominal surgery two years earlier—high-stepped 36 yards into the end zone for a 14–0 lead.

The Bruins never recovered as USC waltzed to a 27–0 victory. The comeback was complete. The Trojans had gone from 1–4—their worst start in four decades—to an improbable 6–5. Soon after, they accepted an invitation to play Utah in the Las Vegas Bowl on Christmas Day.

"To come back from where we were," fullback Charlie Landrigan marveled, lingering on the field after the UCLA win. "Who would believe it?"

———

Did anyone notice Troy Polamalu talking to himself? Could fans see it on television? Did his teammates know?

Between plays, Polamalu had a habit of whispering a quick prayer, asking that no great harm come to himself or anyone else on the field. This request made a certain degree of sense given his shy and deeply religious nature. "There's a very fine line in football," he explained in a voice so quiet as to be inaudible. "You don't want to go out there and break some guy's neck."

Yet, once the ball was snapped, the strong safety turned as wild as the curls of black hair that flowed down over his shoulders. No one played with more ferocity or disregard for personal well-being, and no one deserved more credit for the team's sudden reversal of fortune. Polamalu had helped spark USC's turnaround with an uncanny instinct for the ball, usually followed by a concussive hit. "Kind of like an assassin," one of his teammates said. "He's really quiet . . . and then he turns into a beast."

This dichotomy—the serene fused with the violent—in some ways mirrored the shifting influences of his youth. After spending his earliest years in a rough Southern California neighborhood, a part of Santa Ana riddled by gangs, Polamalu fled to remote Tenmile, Oregon, where he lived with an aunt and uncle. There, he learned woodworking and furniture-making and—coming from a large Samoan family of athletes—he played football. Hardly anyone noticed the kid at tiny Douglas High, especially not when a thigh injury shortened his senior season, but his uncle, former Trojan full-back Kennedy Pola, put in a good word.

Polamalu joked that he was probably the least-recruited player on the field when he arrived at USC. The only way to succeed, he figured, was to outwork everyone else. Before long, the coaches noticed that he always stayed after practice to work on technique or run extra sprints. Paul Hackett made him a starter in 2000, his sophomore season, and he finished second on the team with 83 tackles. Then came Carroll, who had a history of designing his NFL defenses around his safeties, guys such as Ronnie Lott and Lawyer Milloy. He did the same at USC. "That made Troy our centerpiece," associate head coach DeWayne Walker said. "He's our guy." Polamalu had to be versatile, sometimes dropping into coverage, other times creeping up to help that undersized front seven against the run. Asked to do so much, he needed to restrain his preternatural intensity, stifling the urge to simply charge after the ball on every play.

"At times, I felt like, man, I needed to do something special," he said. "I'd take my shot, and half the time I'd miss."

Once the 20-year-old learned to play under control, the game began to flow to him and, for all his bashfulness, he developed a knack for the dramatic. First came a blocked punt against Stanford, then an interception return for a touchdown at Washington. Against Notre Dame, he recovered a fumble that led to a score. In the victory over Oregon State, coaches designed a play to free him on the punt rush, and he responded by deflecting the ball into the end zone where a teammate recovered it. "You can put guys in position to make plays, but not everyone comes through," Carroll said.

In the final two weeks of the 2001 regular season, Polamalu returned an interception for a touchdown against Cal and blocked yet another punt against UCLA. That made for three interceptions, three blocked punts, two forced fumbles, and a fumble recovery to go with what would eventually be a team-high 118 tackles. And that made him USC's first All-American safety in more than a decade. Carroll ranked him among the best he had coached, college or pro, and Utah certainly noticed. "When we watch film, everywhere we look he's in the picture," offensive guard Ed Ta'amu said.

If there was anything that made Polamalu more uncomfortable than all the attention he was receiving—"I hate to get an award that separates me from the team," he said of being named All-American—it was spending the holidays in a place known as Sin City. On the team's first night in town for the Las Vegas Bowl, he walked around the Strip for only a short time before heading back to his hotel room. Neon lights and gambling held scant allure for a young man who preferred to read scripture.

Christmas Day, arriving chilly and clear, put him back in his element. He had the game of his life against Utah, setting a bowl record with 12 solo tackles. Setting another one with 20 total tackles. And it should have been enough to win.

———

There was no curfew that first night in Las Vegas. Carroll was in Florida to watch his son, Brennan, play for Pittsburgh in the Tangerine Bowl, so the USC players checked into the MGM Grand, then headed out to prowl the Strip until all hours or, as receiver Kareem Kelly put it, to "get Las Vegas out of our system." It must not have worked because, as the week wore on, many of the upperclassmen—those who could gamble legally—continued to hit the casinos.

This was Carroll's first bowl game in decades, and he hoped to strike a balance between letting his guys have fun and getting them ready to play. Hovering in the background was some bad history. For the Trojans, it seemed to be "Rose Bowl or bust"—if they didn't make it to Pasadena, they often came out flat in lesser games. The 1982 Fiesta Bowl. The 1987 Citrus Bowl. The 1992 Freedom Bowl. There were other examples. Some of the veterans—including Sultan McCullough and Malaefou MacKenzie—had been on the 1998 squad that lost to Texas Christian in the Sun Bowl.

"We want them to enjoy what they've earned," said Walker, the associate head coach. "However, we are here for a reason."

Utah took a markedly different approach, spending the first part of the week in a sleepy retirement town called St. George, about two hours north, safely across the Utah border. "There's nowhere to go," coach Ron McBride explained. "No distractions." Once in Las Vegas, he continued to keep his team on a short rein.

The regular season had not ended well for the Utes, who had lost their final two games. The odds makers had them as slight underdogs, figuring that Polamalu and the rest of the USC defense could keep their ground-oriented attack from scoring too often. That part was pretty much right. What the experts had failed to consider was Utah's nationally ranked defense.

When game day came around, the Utes blitzed early and often, especially on first and second down. The USC coaches were taken by surprise if only because they had not seen much blitzing in film of Utah's previous games. Chow's plan to control the clock with passes was utterly disrupted because every time Palmer looked up, he saw a rusher—if not two—busting through his beleaguered line. "They were bringing so many guys," he said. The result? Big losses on sacks, lots of third-and-long. At the end of the first quarter, USC had a stunning minus-30 yards in total offense.

Meanwhile, the Utes sent their two big running backs—223-pound Dameon Hunter and the even larger 230-pound Adam Tate—into the line again and again. Late in the first quarter, Tate bounced off a tackler and ran three yards into the end zone. In the second quarter, Hunter helped get his team into position for a field goal and a 10–0 lead. As McBride would later say, pinning a simple explanation on his simple strategy, "We controlled the line of scrimmage today."

The Trojans showed a glimmer of life in the third quarter as Chow adjusted the offense, calling for more runs and shorter throws to counter the blitz. Palmer completed a few passes, and Sunny Byrd finished the 80-yard drive with a short touchdown run. A missed extra point left the score 10–6. The defense was inspired, finding ways to keep Utah from scoring again, the stage set for a comeback. "You kept thinking, *Who's gonna make a play?*" Carroll said. But as quickly as the offense had emerged, it slipped back into hiding, the Trojans going nowhere through a scoreless fourth quarter. Utah took over with 5:43 remaining and ran out the clock on a tough, grinding drive. The final statistics showed USC with 151 yards of total offense, its worst output in five years, and an embarrassing one yard on the ground.

"Sluggish?" Carroll snapped. "We had nothing going on."

His players sat in a cramped locker room, shaking their heads, struggling to explain. "I couldn't have predicted us coming out like that," Landrigan said. Anyone who didn't know the score could have seen the result just as plainly on their faces—the dark red lump on the bridge of Polamalu's nose, the shiner forming under Kelly's right eye. "We just got outplayed," the receiver said. "Bottom line."

———

Chris Carlisle viewed the game of football from a slightly different angle. As a strength coach, he believed there was a direct correlation between repetitions in the weight room and points on the scoreboard. Sweat equaled success. So after Las Vegas, when the players eventually returned to Heritage Hall for another winter of off-season training, he told them, "There's only one way, one tempo—that's full speed."

Carlisle was talking about a football program that could easily have remained stalled in mediocrity after such a disheartening loss.

He was talking about the commitment required to keep pushing forward. And when it came to commitment, no one questioned the man. "What he has been through is 50 times worse than anything I can go through," McCullough said. "If I am running and hot and feeling like I am going to collapse, that is *nothing*."

A year earlier, Carlisle had been working as an assistant at Tennessee, helping the Volunteers prepare for the Southwestern Bell Cotton Bowl, when he felt chest pains and broke into a sweat. An emergency-room doctor said his gall bladder would have to be removed. And one more thing. "Is your wife here?" he asked. Carlisle knew it was serious. Though fit and strong at 39, he had been diagnosed with Hodgkin's disease. At the time, USC and another major college program had expressed interest in hiring him. The other school never called back, but Carroll did not hesitate to offer him the job. "That meant a lot," Carlisle said.

The first winter was grueling, working with the Trojans all week, catching a red-eye flight to Knoxville for chemotherapy on Friday mornings. He slept all of Saturday, then got back on the plane to be on campus by Monday morning. When chemotherapy ended, USC doctors started him on radiation every weekday for a month, the treatment burning his esophagus, making it difficult to speak, yet he never missed work. "The nausea from the chemotherapy and the exhaustion from the radiation, when they started getting to me, I drew energy from the team," he said. "The team kept showing up day after day. Nobody quit on me. . . . In my mind, they were part of the healing process."

By February 2002 Carlisle was cancer-free and feeling good, but he worried that his second off-season at USC might be difficult in another way. Every inch of progress the team had made could be lost if the players did not come back motivated—fully committed—for their workouts. As it turned out, there was no reason to worry. "As soon as we got into winter conditioning . . . we got inspired," Holmes said. "That was a real turning point."

Conquest

Just like in practice, where no one ever walked, the pace in the weight room was nonstop. The bar never rested—when one player finished, another stepped right in. Workouts that once took three hours were done in half the time and, after a full year, the results were beginning to show. The number of players who could bench-press more than 400 pounds had jumped from four to 25. The number who could power-clean more than 300 pounds increased even more, and the big linemen were slimmer. Defensive tackle Mike Patterson said, "You saw yourself getting faster and better."

No one was a better example than Patterson. He had arrived at USC the previous fall at a pudgy 320 pounds, a freshman who could not go more than a few minutes before running out of gas. Carroll wondered, "Who's this guy you're bringing me?" But defensive line coach Ed Orgeron stuck by the kid. There was leverage and hip flexibility in that low-slung body, and quick hands that could frustrate blockers. "There was no way you could simulate his speed and quickness," Orgeron said. "He always had what I call that quick twitch." It had been Carlisle's job to find an athlete under the baby fat.

Although Patterson would never be svelte, his weight dropped to 285 and, during the winter after the Las Vegas Bowl, he became more and more the player Orgeron had envisioned. It seemed there *was* a direct correlation. Rather than lose hope, the Trojans looked at the weight they were lifting, the times they were running, and truly believed the team was headed in the right direction. "Guys realized what [Carroll] was saying," Holmes explained. "They saw the results, and they really bought into it."

The trip back from Las Vegas had been awful for the coaches. They were angry and embarrassed. Worst of all, there was no real chance to take a break, to get away from the game for a while and let their emotions settle. "We had to suck it up and go right back out recruiting," Orgeron recalled. "We had to do a great job of selling."

Lane Kiffin, the receivers coach, hopped on yet another cross-country flight to Tampa. He had the unenviable task of trying to steal Mike Williams, a specimen of a 6'5" receiver, away from the Florida schools. Closer to home, other assistants got in their cars and drove around Southern California, tending to the local prospects.

January was a critical period in the recruiting game, especially the way USC now played it. The Trojans were not afraid to go after the very best prospects, the type who had lots of offers from which to choose and waited until the last minute to decide. While the program had wrapped up a number of talented players—Darnell Bing, Manuel Wright, Justin Wyatt—others still hung in the balance. As national signing day in February drew closer, it was an all-or-nothing proposition.

Among the biggest fish was Winston Justice, an offensive tackle who could conceivably step right in and bolster that ailing line. The USC coaches kept hearing that he was leaning toward UCLA, but they had an advantage because Justice played on the same Long Beach Poly team as Bing and Wright. "Me and Winston were arguing," Wright said. "He was talking about UCLA, and I was talking about USC." The big lineman eventually came around. No such assurances were forthcoming from two other recruits, Lorenzo Booker and Hershel Dennis.

Booker and Dennis ranked as the top running backs in the state and, privately, Carroll knew there was no way both of them would commit to the same school. But as the clock ticked down, he had to juggle both, hoping to get one. The way the system works, recruits can change their minds until the moment they fax a signed letter of intent to their chosen school, so the USC coaches continued to work the phones, talking to the kids or their parents or aunts or cousins— anyone who would listen. At one point during this frenzied process,

Carroll looked up and asked, "Isn't this fun?" Several members of his staff recalled thinking he was crazy.

Finally, on the night before signing day, it appeared certain that Booker had been lost to Florida State. Carroll made a decision. He called Dennis, who had pretty much decided on Oregon, and told the young back to forget about Booker, *he* was USC's top priority. Kennedy Pola, the running backs coach, also got on the line to make a pitch to the kid. Their last-second pleas worked. Dennis recalled, "I just had a good feeling about what they were telling me."

With Williams signing as well, the national experts ranked USC's recruiting class in the top 10 that winter. "A remarkable effort," said Allen Wallace, publisher of *SuperPrep* magazine. "USC was on the precipice of losing the most significant parts of this class, but the staff basically made it happen." As Carroll put it, "We ended the day with a whoop and a holler." But there wasn't much time for celebrating. The loss to Utah had left him frustrated about the offense and needing to work things out with Chow.

These were two experienced, intelligent men, both with distinct ideas about how to do their jobs. During their first season together, the line between them had been well-defined. Carroll had his hands full revamping the defense so—while retaining final say on all major decisions, as well as play-calling—he otherwise left his coordinator alone to run the offense. That was about to change.

As Carroll later explained, "I really dove into the offense between years one and two." The first step involved asking Alex Gibbs, then the Denver Bronco offensive line coach, to advise his staff on blocking schemes. Carroll also wanted a change in the passing game, shorter dropbacks and more play-action to deter the rush. It was the first of many times that he would step into Chow's domain and, from that point on, he quickly corrected anyone who suggested this was Chow's offense. "That's really not how it's been," he said later. Was there tension between the men? Chow would always remain deferential, saying, "Let's keep in mind that this isn't my offense, this is Pete Carroll's offense." Carroll acknowledged, "Norm has been incredibly easy to work with and compliant in dealing with me and my craziness and the way I do stuff and coming out and making it hard on him at times."

Regardless of what happened between the coaches, the team looked sharp on the practice field that spring of 2002. The revamped ground game was clicking with what coaches called a "big-little" philosophy. No more hesitating in the backfield, looking to break a long run and risking a two-yard loss. The ball carriers were told to hit the hole fast and get "big-little" gains of three or four yards. "We needed to develop our style of running the football," Carroll said. "Obviously, our chances have been enhanced by the tail-back situation we have."

The final scrimmage that spring featured Justin Fargas twisting and breaking through tackles for 111 yards. The former Southern California high school star had gone off to Michigan, suffered a string of injuries, and transferred back home. Now he seemed ready to make good on all that potential. At the same time, Sultan McCullough had recovered from his abdominal injury and was eager to keep the starting spot. Palmer looked significantly more comfortable with the simplified passing attack.

"No one's guessing anymore," Holmes said. "We know where to go."

CHAPTER 9

The Golden Boy

T he ball left Carson Palmer's hand in a high arc, sailing across the afternoon sky, hanging there long enough for a stadium full of fans to hold their breath, as if the future of USC football hung in the balance.

It was the fall of 1998, and Palmer had already been designated as a savior. Fans and the media clamored for him the moment he arrived on campus with that square jaw framing an easy grin, a casual winner's attitude. Even the new coach, Paul Hackett, hinted that this golden-haired, golden-armed kid from Orange County might lead the program to better days. The 6'4" freshman was so impressive during his first training camp—uncanny strength, poise, and mechanics—that minutes before the season opener against Purdue, Hackett informed him that he would play in the third quarter.

This advance notice was supposed to lessen Palmer's anxiety, let the kid watch for a while and prepare himself mentally. At least that's what his coach figured. Still, on an August day with the temperature pushing 110 degrees on the field at the Coliseum, Palmer said, "It was a long half."

The Trojans fell behind early and had to fight their way back. They got a kickoff return for a touchdown, and sophomore quarterback Mike Van Raaphorst—the starter—got them close enough for a field goal to close the gap to 17–10. Slightly more than five minutes remained in the third quarter when the sun-baked crowd started buzzing: Palmer was running onto the field with the offense. Hackett wasted no time baptizing his prodigy, calling for a pass on the first snap.

The ball wobbled and fell incomplete.

Palmer came right back and connected with receiver Mike Bastianelli for nine yards. Two plays later, he dropped back and looked deep downfield. The Purdue defense blitzed, forcing him to side-step a rusher before straightening up and, absolutely flat-footed, lofting a pass directly in front of the USC bench. "I just let it go," he said. Much of the crowd rose from their seats as receiver Larry Parker leaped to snatch the ball, falling to the ground with a 42-yard gain. The stadium erupted.

The Trojans scored a few plays later, the start of a 27–17 come-back victory. But the final score seemed almost incidental to that long pass and the debut of the golden boy. "That might have been the worst thing that ever happened to him," tailback Petros Papadakis said years later. "Because everybody just started to go, 'Oh . . . my . . . God.'"

Through much of the eighties and into the nineties, Bob Johnson was on a hot streak. As the coach at El Toro High in Lake Forest, California, he nurtured one successful passer after another. His son Bret went on to play at UCLA and Michigan State. Steve Stenstrom went to Stanford. After a prolific senior season, Johnson's younger son, Rob, signed to play for USC.

At that point, the coach decided to take a break from high school football. To keep his hand in the game, he tutored young players as a private instructor. One day, he received a phone call from a father who had seen an advertisement in a student sports publication and wanted to know if Johnson could take a look at his son. Johnson recalled that the boy "was tall, thin, and just gangly. He was just a puppy."

Palmer was in seventh grade.

Working with the youngster once a week, and also during camps with other quarterbacks, Johnson focused on fundamentals. "There were no bad habits to correct because he didn't have any habits," Johnson said. "He became very efficient very quickly because of that." The third of Bill and Danna Palmer's four children, Carson had been clutching and throwing a ball around the house from the time he could sit up. By the time he met Johnson, he had already been playing tackle football for two years. By the time he arrived at Santa Margarita High, bolstered by all that tutoring, he was regarded by some as a major college prospect. But his record-setting career at Santa Margarita almost ended as soon as it began.

After his sophomore year, his father received a promotion to a job in New York. The Palmers found a house in Connecticut and, before moving, took Carson back east to attend a three-day football camp with the high school team he was likely to play for. Bill was hoping that his son would come back excited and high-fiving the other players. That wasn't what happened. "All of their linemen are fat kids," Bill remembered Carson saying. "All they did was sit around and eat candy bars." As one of the biggest players at the camp, Carson feared the coaches might turn him into a lineman. The Palmers had to make a choice.

Instead of moving the family, Bill took an apartment in Manhattan and began commuting across country each weekend. A relieved Carson flourished at Santa Margarita, leading his team to a 27–1 record and consecutive championships over the next two seasons. "If he went 30 for 30 during practice, we'd buy pizza for all the staff," said Jim Hartigan, his high school coach. "Those were the kinds of things we'd do to keep him motivated because he was so competitive. Those were the kinds of challenges he loved."

Conquest

The final game of his senior season was the stuff of California high school legend. Facing Tustin and its UCLA-bound running back, DeShaun Foster, Palmer threw for five touchdowns and ran for another as Santa Margarita won, 55–42. "The more pressure there was, the better he would play," Hartigan said. Palmer finished his career with more than 4,600 passing yards and 55 touchdowns.

Miami had offered him a scholarship months earlier and now Notre Dame and Washington were hot on the trail. Colorado coach Rick Neuheisel attended a Santa Margarita game, and Palmer was said to be leaning toward the Buffaloes, if only because one of his teammates, John Minardi, had already committed to them. But the Trojans were also in the mix. Hackett, who had just replaced John Robinson, was installing a West Coast offense similar to the one he had run with Joe Montana in San Francisco and Kansas City. He needed a star quarterback.

———

This time, the freshman got a little more warning. Hackett told Palmer on Tuesday that he would start against Washington, the ninth game of the 1998 season, and told him to keep it a secret the rest of the week. The quarterback still did not know all of the playbook but said, "I was excited. I couldn't wait."

Palmer threw for 279 yards that day and led USC to victory, saying he wasn't nervous at all. Under his command, the Trojans won three of four and earned an invitation to the Sun Bowl. Even with the upset loss to Texas Christian, a forgettable afternoon in which Palmer was sacked six times, expectations were high for the next fall. Hackett said during training camp, "This year it's a totally different attitude on offense. This is a group of men who know what is expected. They know the standard."

The Golden Boy

The Trojans started with victories over Hawaii and San Diego State. Then, in the third week, they traveled to Oregon for their Pacific-10 Conference opener. On the next-to-last play before half-time, the game close, Palmer scrambled out of the pocket. Rumbling toward the sideline, he could have stepped safely out of bounds but chose to lower his shoulder and take on a tackler instead. The resulting collision produced a sickeningly familiar crunch.

Fractured collarbones were nothing new to him. He was so big at birth—more than 10 pounds—that doctors intentionally broke both his clavicles to ensure a safe delivery. At age 10, he broke his left clavicle while playing football with his brother. As a sophomore in high school, he suffered a hairline fracture in the right one. This time, the X-rays confirmed what he already suspected. The right collarbone had snapped again, much worse this time, and the recovery could take weeks, if not months. He was probably done for the season. "Football is my life," Palmer said later. "It's what I do every day, and it was taken away in one little hit."

Hackett watched closely to see how his quarterback would respond. Palmer never complained, but he wasn't as good-natured as before, wasn't joking around in the locker room. During home games, he anxiously roamed the sideline. During away games, he squirmed in front of the television at home, especially when the Trojans blew a 21-point lead and lost 25–24 to Notre Dame. "He was dying," his father said. The doctors had given Palmer a slight chance of recovering in time for the UCLA game, so he focused on that goal. But it did not take long for the shoulder muscles to atrophy. By the time he started physical therapy, he could barely throw the ball, and even a few push-ups left him tired.

The day of the UCLA game, Palmer walked onto the Coliseum field in street clothes and lost it, tears of disappointment in his eyes. "Everybody's fired up and the stadium was going nuts and I was thinking, *This is my game. I should be playing in this game*," he said. USC defeated UCLA 17–7 to end an eight-game losing streak against the Bruins, but it marked a low point for the injured star.

Quietly, he began to wonder about his arm, about whether he would recover his natural throwing motion. For the first time, he worried about his ability to play football.

———

It was a hungry young quarterback who announced his return the next spring by shoving through the gates and sprinting onto Howard Jones Field. This newfound passion continued through summer, through weightlifting and running, into training camp. While some teammates groused about the workload, Palmer pushed himself, attentive at meetings, eager to improve his footwork. "When I got hurt, it gave me a new perspective," he said. "I take every snap like it's my last." There were no more doubts about his arm. "If anything, he's stronger," receiver Marcell Allmond said during camp. "When I'm running a route, I have to get my head around quicker or the ball is going to hit me in the face."

That fall, several preseason magazines put Palmer on their covers, and the university plastered his image, larger-than-life, on billboards throughout Los Angeles. No matter that he had yet to defeat UCLA or win a bowl game. No matter that his 5–3 record as a starter was good but less than spectacular. The "Golden Boy" promotional machine was back in full swing. Palmer never liked that image. He did his best to calm things down, reminding people of all that he had yet to accomplish, and Hackett tried to help with a subtle warning. "He teased us all as a freshman, then misses a year," the coach said. "I don't think he has arrived yet."

Maybe fans should have taken the hint when Palmer started sluggishly, throwing for only 87 yards with an interception against Penn

State. But the Trojans won that game and it was, after all, his first time on the field in almost a year. He came right back against Colorado, completing 25 of 30, including six in a row during a game-winning drive. And he stayed hot against San Jose State as the undefeated Trojans climbed in the national rankings. But the next stretch of games would quickly put a damper on all the hype.

Three interceptions against Oregon State, three against Arizona, and one against Oregon. Two against Stanford and two more against California.

Palmer had thought nothing could be tougher than the season before, watching his teammates lose five in a row. He was wrong. "Now I'm *in* the games and we're losing," he said. "That's an even worse feeling." He was playing behind a shaky offensive line, not much support from the run game, and the team was committing too many needless mistakes, including delay-of-game penalties when the plays came in late. It seemed that whenever USC fell behind, Palmer's competitive instincts—lurking behind that easygoing manner—had him trying to make things happen on his own, trying to manufacture big plays and getting burned. No one doubted his natural talent, but the turnovers raised questions about another part of his game: decision-making. It was an issue that would come to haunt him.

The ninth game of the season brought a short respite against Arizona State, a double-overtime victory in which Palmer guided his team to the winning touchdown. "He was smiling in the huddle like, 'Isn't this fun,'" offensive lineman Brent McCaffrey said. But then came Washington State, an early interception and several wayward passes that started the crowd booing. In the locker room at halftime, Hackett decided to pull his quarterback, saying that, "The team needed a jolt." Van Raaphorst got a cheer when he started the third quarter, but USC lost anyway, dropping into last place in the Pacific-10.

There wasn't much Palmer could say: after 10 games, he had thrown 10 touchdown passes and 16 interceptions. "The quarterback's job is to win the game," he mused. "When we're not winning, you've got to make the switch." The demotion was short-lived. The next day, Hackett announced that Palmer would start against UCLA, holding onto the job by means of a stronger arm and better mobility, if not sheer potential.

The final two weeks were a microcosm of Palmer's career to that point. Against UCLA, he looked dazzling, leading his team to victory with 350 passing yards and four touchdowns. Against Notre Dame, even as he connected on some tough throws, he also had two more interceptions to tie the school record at 18 in a season. The loss put a fitting capper on USC's 5–7 record. "This wasn't the way I wanted to go out," he said.

A few days later, Hackett was fired.

————

There were at least two good reasons to feel excited about the subsequent changes at USC. Although Palmer was circumspect about his troubles—"When you throw 18 interceptions, it's not one thing"— those close to the program knew that he had been caught in a difficult situation between Hackett and the offensive coordinator, Hue Jackson. Now he had a new coach in Pete Carroll and, just as important, a coordinator whose play-calling responsibilities were more clearly defined, all the information coming from one source.

Palmer knew about Norm Chow's success at Brigham Young and North Carolina State and quickly took a liking to him. "He reminds me so much of my dad," he said. "Real conservative. Real mellow." Chow knew about Palmer, too, saying, "I knew some of the history, some of the labels, if you will." During spring practice, the coordinator realized this was as physically gifted a passer as any he had coached in his 28 seasons. Just as big as Philip Rivers and even stronger. If Palmer could run the offense effectively, he might turn out to be the best of all.

"I liked the guy," Chow said. "I just felt he needed some confidence."

Things started well enough in the 2001 season opener against San Jose State but it wasn't long before old ghosts rose to haunt the quarterback. The urge to do too much led to problems the very next week against Kansas State when he took on that pair of tacklers and fumbled away USC's last chance to win the game. "His competitiveness got the best of him," Carroll said. Against Oregon, he set a school record with 419 yards of total offense but had three passes intercepted. And there was that moment at the end when, under pressure, he threw the ball away instead of going down and forcing Oregon to use its final timeout.

Palmer knew what people were thinking. "Decision-making," he said. Carroll preached patience, saying that the learning curve for the position could stretch across five or six years. "He's a guy who is still growing and developing," the new coach said. "We're in that process." Just across town, former UCLA quarterback Cade McNown had shown improvement midway through his college career, a change so sudden and distinct it was compared to flicking on a light bulb. When asked if he felt such a moment coming, Palmer could only say, "I hope. I hope the light bulb is about to go on."

But there were two more interceptions against Stanford, and the team kept losing. Things got so bad that, with USC at 2–5, Carroll and Chow contemplated changing quarterbacks, even telling freshman Matt Leinart to be ready for the next game at Arizona. "You get frustrated as a coach," Chow said. "Pete and I talked about it. If he hadn't done well, we'd make a change. But when you sat back and thought about it you realized it was a dumb thing to do. It was not his fault. It was just the way we were playing."

The late-season comeback—those four straight wins—took some heat off Palmer, but the offense looked dreadful against Utah in the Las Vegas Bowl. The quarterback got battered and threw for only 150 yards. At the end of his junior year, the statistics told a story of utter mediocrity: a record of 16–16 in games he had started, and an even split of 39 touchdowns and 39 interceptions.

There would be no great hype going into the 2002 season. Palmer wouldn't even make the cover of his school's media guide. The Golden Boy had one more season to prove that he was something more than just average.

CHAPTER 10

Turning the Corner

The first game of the season was a big one. A tough Auburn team. National television on a Monday night. Mike Williams, the highly touted freshman, had come to USC because he wanted to play right away, but when he walked out of the tunnel at the Coliseum and caught sight of all those cameras—not to mention more than sixty-three thousand fans—the kid suffered a temporary case of stage fright.

So the coaches wasted no time sending him onto the field, and Carson Palmer promptly threw him a pass. It was the quickest way to get rid of his butterflies. "Exactly what I needed," he said.

The Trojans could not afford to keep their young phenom on the bench or bring him along slowly—they were facing too many difficult questions in the fall of 2002. Was this the team that turned a corner with four straight victories the season before? Or the one that fell flat in the Las Vegas Bowl? Could the quarterback finally make good on his golden boy image? What about the beleaguered offensive line? The answers would come soon because USC faced a schedule front-loaded with nationally ranked teams. Pete Carroll warned, "If we're not a really tied-together, well-executing team, we'll get whipped the first three weeks."

Auburn posed the most immediate threat in the form of Carnell Williams, a load of a running back whose nickname was "Cadillac." As his coach, Tommy Tuberville, said, "There is no cruise control." Against the Trojans, the sophomore showed what he could do right away, gaining nearly 100 yards in the first half, scoring a touchdown, and helping to set up another. The best the USC defense could manage was to force a couple of turnovers, keeping the game close, buying time until they made adjustments against the run. The score was tied, 17–17, midway through the fourth quarter, when Palmer finally took over.

An 18-yard pass to Kareem Kelly. Eight yards to Sunny Byrd. Nine yards to Malaefou MacKenzie. Then, with Auburn on its heels—and maybe a little wobbly from the heat that night—the Trojans changed gears. They ran the ball six times in a row, Palmer going the final yard into the end zone on a sneak. It was a crushing drive, lasting more than eight minutes, and it was good for a 24–17 victory.

"We showed a lot of people that we are going to keep coming," defensive lineman Omar Nazel said. "We showed them that we are going to play until the end."

But that was only the first test. After an easy win at Colorado—the Buffaloes did not live up to their No. 18 ranking—USC traveled to play No. 25 Kansas State in remote Manhattan, Kansas. Palmer had particular reason to be wary of this game, given that the Wildcats had shut him down in a 10–6 loss the season before. "I'm not sure there are many defenses in the Pac-10 that are as good as this one," he said. The big question was Kansas State quarterback Ell Roberson and his ability to play despite an injured hand.

In more ways than one, that chilly night at sold-out KSU Stadium resembled the previous season's game. Again, Roberson befuddled the USC defense, coming off the bench to run for big gains, staking his team to a three-touchdown lead. Again, USC fought back, scoring twice in the fourth quarter to close the gap to 27–20. Again, Palmer had an opportunity to win it with a last-second drive. As time ran down, he drove the Trojans into Kansas State territory.

The 2001 game had been decided in dramatic fashion, Palmer running for a first down, getting sandwiched by tacklers, and fumbling.

This time, any chance for victory ended with a whimper. On fourth and 15, his throw to Keary Colbert sailed high and incomplete. In the locker room afterward, he characteristically took the blame for the loss, but Colbert, sitting a few feet away, would have none of it. He told reporters he ran the wrong route.

A 2–1 start was not exactly what Carroll had hoped for. Still, with fewer mistakes from their quarterback and a little more punch from the ground game, the Trojans had shown the potential to be a different team from seasons past. As their coach said, "We survived . . . all and all, we're ready for the Pac-10." The next week, they went out and proved it, returning to the Coliseum for a 22–0 victory over previously undefeated Oregon State. The win kept USC at No. 18 in the nation. "We are really excited," Carroll said. "We like where we are right now."

———

Four games into the season, Mike Williams had gone from untested to an emerging force on offense, getting lots of playing time, eager to crack the starting lineup. Carroll called him "flashy" and "a raw talent." Williams was not about to disagree. The big kid from Tampa had all the physical tools, the strength and large hands, combined with a self-assurance that bordered on cocky.

Back in high school, he had been on the verge of slipping through the cracks. An unruly 16-year-old living from house to house, suspended one too many times from school. He was taken in by the McCurdys, a white family from the wealthy side of Tampa who knew him because his great-aunt had been their nanny. In the stability of a newfound home, Williams had turned his life around, both as a person and a football player.

Florida athletes tended to stick close to home, and Williams had pretty much decided to play for the Florida Gators up in Gainesville, changing his mind only when their famous coach, Steve Spurrier, took a job with the Washington Redskins. After that, he considered Florida State but flipped through the team's media guide and saw too many freshman and sophomores languishing on the bench, waiting their turn. "It wasn't the place for me," he said.

The Trojans lured him west with their now-familiar promise: *If you're good enough, you can play right away.* Lane Kiffin, the young receivers coach, pointed to defensive lineman Shaun Cody, who had appeared in almost every game the previous season and made several freshman All-America teams. Kiffin even pulled out a notepad and pencil, sketching the routes that Williams would run beside Kelly and Colbert in multiple-receiver sets. Williams said, "I could see where I was going to fit in."

Still, attending school some 3,000 miles from home would not be easy. After a summer on campus, working out beside his new teammates, the teenager wondered about his decision. He was flying back to Tampa for a quick visit with his family and ran into Keyshawn Johnson, the former USC receiver, at Los Angeles International Airport. "He basically told me that when I got out here for school and the season started, the homesickness would totally go away," Williams said. "And he was 100 percent right."

The freshman's comfort level was important to the Trojans in two ways. If USC wanted to attract the best recruits from all over the nation, the coaches needed to tell them, *Look at Mike. He's glad that he came to Los Angeles.* It was a sales pitch they would make to LenDale White, the Colorado prospect, the very next spring. In the meantime, they also got an extremely talented athlete.

Williams' first catch against Auburn went for nine yards. The defensive back hit him and it wasn't so different from practice, where teammates such as Troy Polamalu and DeShaun Hill "are trying to kill you," he said. He finished with four receptions that day, seven the next week against Colorado. The Kansas State game had been humbling, Williams letting several passes slip through his hands and finishing with only one catch for 11 yards, but the slump did not last long.

The next week, at home against Oregon State, he came back to the huddle and insisted there was no way the defensive back across the line could cover him. Sure enough, Williams caught a pair of touchdown passes that day and served notice to the rest of the Pacific-10 Conference. "He's a big target," Mike Bellotti, the Oregon coach would later say. "He can catch the ball and make the run after the catch."

Four games into the season, Williams was already beginning to overshadow Kelly and draw comparisons to that guy he had met in the airport, the one who had been an All-American and the first player chosen in the 1996 NFL draft. It was becoming clear that USC had something special.

———

Just when it seemed like the Trojans were on a roll, surviving that early season stretch, they went up to Washington State and blew a game they should have won. Palmer threw an interception in the end zone. Ryan Killeen bounced a field goal attempt off the upright and missed an extra-point. The Cougars came back to tie the score in regulation, then won, 30–27, in overtime.

Suddenly, the Trojans were 3–2 and facing a critical juncture in their season. Those troubling questions they seemed to have answered in the first four weeks were back again. Was this just another mediocre team? Was a losing streak on the way? "All of a sudden we were back to having to prove ourselves," Cody said. Next on the schedule was California. So feeble the season before, the Golden Bears were rebounding with a new coach, Jeff Tedford, and strong-armed quarterback Kyle Boller. They had a 4–2 record and—

coming into the Coliseum—quickly proved it was no fluke, opening a big lead in the second quarter. Then came a play that changed the course of the game, if not more.

Down by 18 points, the Trojans had a chance to close the gap, facing third down at Cal's 6-yard line. As Palmer dropped back to pass, the pocket collapsed and forced him to scramble to his right. Kelly spotted his quarterback on the move and began gliding across the back of the end zone with Cal safety Nnamdi Asomugha—and an official—trailing behind. Asomugha recalled, "I saw Carson's eyes get real big. I knew he was going to throw Kareem's way, but I thought, *There's no way.*" The low pass appeared to skip off the ground before Kelly got control and the defender thought, *Oh good. He missed it.*

Not so fast. The back judge ruled a touchdown, prompting the referee to call for a conference. A replay on the Coliseum video board clearly showed an incompletion. The final ruling? Touchdown. "I saw the ball hit the ground," Palmer said later. "But I also saw the ref's arms go up—and I wasn't going to complain about that." Neither was Kelly. He would later acknowledge that the most important catch of his career wasn't a catch at all but, on that day, he was merely following a tip from a former coach: if you get a ball near the ground, immediately roll over and show it to the official.

The phantom touchdown started USC on a run, paving the way for a 30–28 comeback victory. The win came at a cost—Cody, the defensive lineman, suffered a season-ending knee injury—but the 19th-ranked Trojans had some momentum and, with the schedule easing up a little, were poised for their first bona fide run at the Rose Bowl in almost a decade. Kelly said a year later, "That play right there was our whole season."

After a comfortable victory over Washington, the team headed north to dreaded Autzen Stadium, where Palmer was winless against Oregon over the course of his career. "I definitely have some unfinished business," he said. He took care of it with a school-record 448 passing yards and five touchdowns, guiding his team to a 44–33 win that was equally satisfying for the receivers. Before the season began, Oregon had put a huge billboard featuring its receiving corps on the side of a downtown Los Angeles hotel. It was part of a nationwide marketing campaign, the Pacific Northwest school hoping to elevate its image, and it had not gone over well at USC. In fact, the Trojans had put a copy of it on their playbook that week. "We took that personally because we felt that our three were better than their three," Kiffin said. Williams exacted revenge with a huge performance, catching 13 passes for 226 yards and two touchdowns.

The next two games brought victories over Stanford and Arizona State. USC now had an 8–2 record and a lofty No. 7 ranking, with only UCLA and Notre Dame left to play. "The opportunity is there—it's on the table," Palmer said. "We don't have to worry about who's winning, who's losing, and what our BCS ranking is. We just have to go out and keep winning. If we do that, we'll be in good position."

He was almost right.

———

Hardly anyone knew that Justin Fargas would be the starting tailback that day against Oregon. Even some of his teammates were surprised when he showed up in the huddle before the first snap. It was a moment that, as Fargas put it, was "a long time coming."

Back in the late nineties, he had been a schoolboy hero at Notre Dame High, only 25 minutes up the freeway from USC. With an angular build and smooth running style, he had made the spectacular look routine. One play, in particular, was part of the local folklore: somersaulting over a pileup at the line, Fargas landed on his feet and kept running 35 yards to the end zone. Everyone expected the senior to perform this sort of magic for the hometown Trojans, but when the program fired John Robinson and brought in pass-oriented Paul Hackett, Fargas went to Michigan instead. Thus began a four-year odyssey.

His college career got off to a fast start in 1998, the freshman working his way into the rotation and rushing for 120 yards in ankle-deep mud at Northwestern. Michigan coach Lloyd Carr called him "a real bright spot . . . that kid showed a lot." Then came a brutal injury against Wisconsin, his right leg so badly shattered that doctors pondered amputating the foot. They tried reassembling the bones with titanium rods and, when that didn't work, had to rebreak the leg and start over, this time inserting metal plates. Fargas needed almost two years to recover and, by the time he returned in 2000, the Wolverines had talented running backs Anthony Thomas and Chris Perry above him on the depth chart. After a brief attempt at playing in the secondary, it became clear, he said, "I wasn't going to accomplish my dreams at Michigan."

Carroll had taken over at USC that winter, so Fargas and his father, Antonio—the actor who played "Huggy Bear" in the seventies television series *Starsky and Hutch*—met with the new coach to discuss a transfer. Antonio said his son "needed to be close to home . . . to come back and pick up the pieces." Carroll agreed, and Justin made the switch immediately, leaving Michigan even as the team was preparing for the Citrus Bowl. He enrolled in classes at USC and, though NCAA rules prohibited him from playing the 2001 season, wasted no time establishing himself as a star on the practice field.

Something about the young man had changed. There was an element of ferocity now, and the very sound of him running in scrimmages—a cacophony of grunting, feet churning, the clack of shoulder pads as he confronted one tackler after another—caused teammates and coaches to stop and watch from other parts of the field. "He was breaking tackles and doing everything he could,"

Cody recalled. "He's a wild man." On the final day of spring practice in 2002, Fargas carried 12 times for 111 yards.

It seemed the stage was set for him to start the next fall, but there was another setback, a strained hamstring in training camp, and Sultan McCullough kept the job. Fargas was growing desperate. Although Carroll intended to keep him on the sideline until he was free of injury, the senior coaxed running back coach Kennedy Pola into sending him in for one play against Colorado, a four-yard gain. Carroll immediately ordered the equipment managers to confiscate his helmet. Fargas said sheepishly, "I'm just happy to get that first carry out of the way."

Maybe the biggest play of his career came five weeks later against Washington. The 13-yard touchdown run, late in a blowout victory, wasn't nearly as impressive as the way teammates mobbed him afterward. This show of emotion struck Carroll, who quietly decided to start Fargas the next week because of "a gut feeling . . . sometimes they work, sometimes they don't."

This one did. Fargas rushed for 139 yards against Oregon, including a 15-yard touchdown that broke the game open in the third quarter, and it was something of an understatement when he called that day the highlight of his college career. The Trojans had a new star in the backfield, a guy who later explained, "The more you carry the ball, the more confident you get."

Even if you have to wait four years.

———

In mid-November, USC sent two emissaries—senior associate athletic directors Daryl Gross and Steve Lopes—on a plane heading east. They stopped in New Orleans to speak with Sugar Bowl officials, then flew to Miami to meet with the Orange Bowl committee.

Conquest

For the first time in more than a decade, the Trojans had reached this late point in the season with a No. 7 ranking, only one game behind Washington State in the race for the Rose Bowl. Short of making it to Pasadena, they stood a good chance of being invited to one of the prestigious bowl games that comprised the bowl championship series—thus the visits by Gross and Lopes, who did not want their team to be overlooked. As Gross said, "We just wanted to get out in front of it and let them know we're here."

In the meantime, the Trojans still had two big games left, starting with No. 25 UCLA. The Bruins, mindful of their embarrassing shutout loss the previous season, figured they would need to play almost flawlessly to score an upset. Any hopes for such a performance were quickly dashed.

With a sold-out crowd at the Rose Bowl, UCLA fumbled the opening kickoff and, on the very next play, Chow looked to exploit something he had seen in game films. UCLA cornerback Matt Ware appeared susceptible to double moves, so the offensive coordinator called a pass play. As Kelly explained, "I gave [Ware] a hard step inside, he bit on it, and there it was." The 34-yard touchdown play made the score 7–0 just 16 seconds into the game. On the next two possessions, Colbert added a long touchdown catch, and Fargas scored on a short run.

UCLA coach Bob Toledo called it "a world of hurt," his team on the way to a 52–21 loss. The Bruins' running game went nowhere, and their quarterbacks were sacked five times. Their fans began filing out of the stadium so early that, on the USC sideline, coaches joked that somebody must have been giving out pizza in the parking lot. "To beat UCLA so convincingly twice in a row, that's unheard of," Palmer said. The senior quarterback, who threw four touchdown passes, had another thought, *I hope the BCS is looking at us.*

The No. 6 Trojans could not have asked for a more perfect stage, concluding the regular season against No. 7 Notre Dame at the

Coliseum. Two great teams, plenty of national implications, and an interesting subplot. Ever since that big day against Oregon, Palmer had been working his way into the Heisman Trophy picture. "Just look at his numbers and the schedule we have played," Carroll said. "He has to be one of the top favorites for this award from this point on."

Palmer stated his case emphatically the Saturday after his coach spoke up. With the Irish leading 6–0 on a pair of field goals, he put on a torrid display, throwing two touchdown passes to Mike Williams in the second quarter, one to Malaefou MacKenzie in the third, and another to MacKenzie in the fourth. By the time he came out of the game with two minutes remaining, the senior had passed for 425 yards against a defense that ranked in the top 20 in every category. Two years after tying a school record with 18 interceptions, he was on his way to setting another one with 33 touchdown passes and was the Pacific-10 Conference's all-time leader in total offense.

"He was able to pick us apart," Irish linebacker Courtney Watson said. "We weren't able to slow him down."

And USC won 44–13.

The Trojans had a 10-2 record and an outside chance at the Rose Bowl, even if it meant rooting for UCLA against Washington State the next week. This predicament led to something probably never seen before on Howard Jones Field: after practice one day, the offensive linemen gathered to cheer "Go Bruins." It didn't work— Washington State won and clinched a trip to Pasadena.

At that point, USC figured to be headed for the Sugar Bowl against third-ranked Georgia. But then came the kind of twist that only the BCS could produce, Orange Bowl officials finagling a very Pasadena-like matchup by inviting the Trojans to play Iowa of the Big Ten. Kirk Ferentz, the Hawkeyes coach, called it a Rose Bowl "on the wrong coast."

"A bowl is a bowl, and I'm happy to be in one of the biggest," junior Marcell Allmond said. "I just want to play football."

Conquest

It wasn't hard to pick the moment—or maybe two of them—when Carson Palmer turned himself into a verifiable Heisman contender.

The first was a play against UCLA that wasn't a touchdown or even a pass. With the ball on the Bruins 23-yard line, he took off running and, like so many times before, threw his body toward the end zone. Hit hard, the big quarterback cartwheeled and crashed to the ground. Although he fell one yard short of a score, the fans cheered his tenacity, and the play was shown again and again on highlight shows. As *Los Angeles Times* columnist Bill Plaschke wrote, "For a Heisman Trophy candidate whose résumé lacked only a single defining moment, that was it."

Then came the extraordinary night against Notre Dame, completing one pass after another as a nationwide audience, if not a few Heisman voters, watched on television. The point was clear: Palmer had been given an opportunity and had delivered.

Still, there were so many bad memories to overcome, those mediocre seasons and all those interceptions. Even after he was named an All-American and won the Unitas Award as the nation's top senior passer, the laid-back young man flew off to the Heisman ceremony in New York with guarded expectations. "It's such a far-fetched goal," he said. "You can't really picture yourself up on the podium."

On the evening of December 14, that is exactly where Palmer ended up. In a ballroom converted into a television studio, he accepted the bronze trophy as the 68th Heisman winner and said, "My heart's about to come out of my shirt." He had easily out-distanced the other four finalists, drawing the most votes in all but one region of the country, making him the first West Coast player to win the award since USC's Marcus Allen in 1981. "A lot of people have talked about the East Coast bias," he said. "I think this kind of answers that." A quarterback had joined the pantheon of runners at "Tailback U."

The next 48 hours passed in a whirlwind. There were photo sessions, poses beside the trophy, and a morning visit to the set of *NFL Today*, where analyst and former Cincinnati Bengals quarterback Boomer Esiason speculated that his old team might take Palmer with the first pick of the upcoming draft. "Have you ever been to Cincinnati?" he asked. "Guess what, son. You're going." The next night, Palmer was guest of honor at a $600-a-plate, black-tie dinner. Seventeen former winners—including Mike Garrett and Charles White—were among those in attendance who gave him a standing ovation.

With each appearance, every speech he made, Palmer seemed to grow in confidence, more commanding, more at ease. At the dinner, he let the room in on some of his personal thoughts: "I was sitting there and was kind of trying to put things in perspective, and I realized I'm just some punk college kid in a rented tuxedo rubbing elbows with Archie Griffin and shaking Earl Campbell's hand. I don't know when it's going to wear off, but I hope it never does because this is such a cool feeling."

There was one more night to party in New York with his fiancée Shaclyn Fernandes and his younger brother Jordan, a quarterback at Texas–El Paso. Then came a morning flight to Los Angeles. It was time to get back to work.

———

The hamstring had been sore all season and now it was only getting worse. As Troy Polamalu struggled through warm-ups before the final and biggest game of his college career—the Orange Bowl against Iowa—it was obvious that he would not be able to play without a painkilling injection. The toughest athlete on the USC roster limped off the field to find a doctor.

Conquest

A few minutes later, teammate Jason Leach was sitting beside him in the locker room.

"I can't feel my leg," Polamalu said.

"What?" Leach replied. "Naw, go run that off."

When Polamalu tried to run, his knee locked. When he stopped, his ankle turned. The team doctor had inadvertently struck a nerve while administering the injection, leaving only numbness. "I said I would never take a shot until my senior year and would especially take one if it's the last game because, to me, there is no tomorrow," Polamalu said. "I regret that decision." It was an unexpected setback in what had already been an unexpected month.

The Trojans were playing in South Florida only because of the unfathomable machinations of the BCS. The ranking system had been created to identify the No. 1 and No. 2 teams at the end of the season, but it encompassed more than one game. Four major bowls were involved—the Rose, Fiesta, Sugar, and Orange—each taking a turn hosting the title game while the other three picked from the remaining teams. The Orange, because of its spot in the pecking order, had been able to steal USC away from the Sugar.

The week before the game, Carroll reminded his players of how far they had come since the Las Vegas Bowl only a year earlier. "That game, that whole thing, started this off," he said. Darrell Rideaux, the cornerback, agreed, "The best thing that could have happened to us, I hate to say, was losing that bowl game because it kept guys hungry." Shortly after Christmas, the Trojans settled in for what they hoped would be a week of quiet workouts at a small college north of Miami. Little did they know.

O. J. Simpson walked onto the practice field five days before the game, smiling, dressed in black sweatpants and a golf shirt. Normally, everyone would have been thrilled to see a former Heisman winner. Simpson, however, was a highly controversial figure, not so far removed from the trial in which he had been acquitted of the brutal murders of his ex-wife, Nicole Simpson, and her friend, Ronald Goldman. He had been invited not by USC officials but by Fargas, who had known him for years. "He's such a big part of the tradition at 'SC and a lot of guys have never seen him," the tailback said.

The players, many of whom were in grade school at the time of the murders, greeted Simpson with handshakes and hugs. Palmer chatted with him, and Carroll tried to put the best possible spin on the situation. "Our guys hold a Heisman Trophy winner in the highest regard," he said. "For them to get a chance to see him and visit with him was very special." Back in Los Angeles, angry fans inundated the athletic department and local media outlets with critical letters.

The final surprise for USC—after O.J. and Polamalu's ill-fated injection—came on the opening kickoff, which Iowa returned 100 yards for a touchdown. The stadium, awash in the black and gold of the Hawkeyes, went wild. But the Trojans still had a tough defense and they still had Palmer. When he tossed a 65-yard bomb to Kelly on the next possession, setting up a short touchdown run by Fargas, the game settled down. The teams played back and forth for a while and, if there was a turning point, it was subtle. At the end of the first half, Iowa was lining up for a field-goal attempt when defensive lineman Bernard Riley noticed a gap in the line. "One of their guards was loose," Riley said. "I just got in there and put up my hand." The blocked kick kept the score at 10–10 and, after a halftime fireworks display, USC came out with some pyrotechnics of its own.

An 18-yard touchdown pass to Mike Williams. A 50-yard touchdown run by Fargas, who explained, "I just kept my eyes on the end zone and turned on the speed." Then a long, patient drive capped by McCullough's five-yard run. Three straight possessions and three straight touchdowns.

After so much struggle in his career, Fargas ran for 122 yards and two scores. After so much frustration, Palmer passed for 303 yards and proved his worth as a Heisman winner. The defense stifled Iowa, keeping speedy quarterback Brad Banks off-balance all night and limiting the Hawkeyes' best running back, Fred Russell, to about a third of his 122-yard average. By the time the smoke cleared, USC had a convincing 38–17 victory, and Ferentz, the Iowa coach, could only shrug: "What can I say? They have a great football team."

The Trojans finished at No. 4 in the polls, although some in the media suggested they might have been playing the best football in the nation by season's end. They had the best quarterback and one of the hottest coaches in the game. Finally, it seemed, they had answered all the questions. All but one.

As Williams put it, "The only thing that can feel better than this is if we're playing for the national championship next year."

CHAPTER 11

The Ugly Duckling

The boy was chubby. No getting around it. He was also born with a condition known as *strabismus*, which caused his eyes to cross. Even after surgery, that meant wearing Coke-bottle glasses all through elementary school. His mother used to read him the story of the ugly duckling, saying that, "Someday you're going to be a prince. Mark my words."

To which a young Matt Leinart replied, "Mom, you don't know what you're talking about."

Years later, it would seem as if Leinart had been sent to USC by central casting, tall and good looking, cool under pressure, all the right ingredients for a star quarterback. The question was: could he emerge from a pack of contenders vying to replace Carson Palmer? Would he be the one to lead the Trojans to a national championship? It was a high-stakes scenario that must have seemed so far removed from his childhood.

The eye problem stuck with Leinart through his middle school years. "Wearing glasses was one thing, being cross-eyed was another," he recalled. "That really kind of stunk, to be blunt." Although he showed promise as an athlete from the very beginning, the other boys and girls teased him. "Kids can be tough," he said. Eventually, the youngest of Bob and Linda Leinart's two sons hit a growth spurt, his baby fat melting away, and a subsequent eye surgery allowed him to put the glasses aside for good. By the time he reached Mater Dei High in 1997, Leinart stood lean and tall, well over six feet.

People around his hometown of Santa Ana knew him as an up-and-coming pitcher, a left-hander with a wicked curve and a fastball that scouts had clocked in the mideighties. But Bruce Rollinson, the football coach at Mater Dei, heard something else about the incoming freshman, murmurs from parents and school supporters. "They all talked about how great he threw it as a flag football player," Rollinson said. Mater Dei had one of the most powerful and long-standing football programs in the state. John Huarte had played there in the early sixties before going to Notre Dame and winning the Heisman Trophy. More recently, the Monarchs had won a string of regional titles and two mythical national championships in the nineties. Still, Leinart wasn't sure he wanted to play football. The private Catholic school charged a participation fee for each sport, and his father told him, "We're only going to pay for two, so you pick 'em." Baseball was a given—Matt was already practicing with the varsity team. Basketball seemed like it might be fun. Then his older brother stepped in.

Ryan Leinart, a baseball and basketball player in his high school days, had always regretted not trying football. Besides, he figured that if his younger brother attended Mater Dei's freshman football camp over the summer, Matt would make dozens of friends by the time classes began in fall. So Ryan put up the money. And Rollinson got his first glimpse. "I'm thinking, *Hmm, this is a big, old, tall, gangly kid . . .* probably 6'2" and weighed a buck-80," the coach said. "But he had the ability to see the field and had touch on the football."

Leinart was quickly sold on the sport. When camp ended, the Mater Dei coaches advised him to contact a man named Steve Clarkson. A former quarterback—he played for Jack Elway at San Jose State and had a brief stint in the NFL—Clarkson was known as a talented private instructor, a guy who had worked with

The Ugly Duckling

Heisman winner Gino Torretta, among other top quarterbacks. He recalled that Leinart showed up wearing high-top basketball shoes on size-14 feet. "He couldn't find football shoes, so that was the first thing I worked on—getting him football shoes," Clarkson said. At first glance, the teenager appeared to have a good arm. And something else.

"What I loved about him was his work ethic," Clarkson said. "He was one of the first guys there and one of the last to leave."

———

Something in his shoulder felt strange. Leinart noticed it that summer while playing baseball. But tests revealed no major damage, so he played for Mater Dei's freshman football team through the fall and even pitched on weekends in winter league games before having a minor procedure to correct loose ligaments. That's when doctors found damage to the labrum and rotator cuff.

The more-extensive surgery required a long rehabilitation, Leinart was told not to pick up a ball of any kind for at least nine months. "He was depressed, seriously depressed," his father said. Leinart's mother recalled his words, "My career is over. My life is over." Doctors suspected he might never throw a fastball again—at least, not in the eighties—but they told Rollinson that he might return even stronger as a quarterback. "I thought, 'Well, that's pretty good news because he threw it pretty good as a freshman,'" the coach said.

When the next football season came around, Leinart was still recovering and had to watch practices from the sideline. Finally, in the summer of 1999, he returned to workouts, and the doctors were right. "The first thing we noticed was, Holy Moly, look at this thing coming out of his hand," Rollinson said. That fall, Leinart shared the quarterback job with Matt Grootegoed through training camp and the first four games before taking over full-time. He passed for 2,400 yards and 15 touchdowns while leading the Monarchs to a co-championship. One season was all it took to attract interest from a number of major college programs. Leinart verbally committed to USC, choosing the Trojans over Michigan because he liked Paul Hackett and running backs coach Kennedy Pola, a Mater Dei alumnus.

His future apparently set, the teenager focused on the approaching season. The tribulations of childhood had made him easygoing by nature, a roll-with-the-punches type, but by the fall of 2000 he had grown quite passionate about football, as evidenced by his reaction to Rollinson's pregame speeches. "We had to be careful because Matt might end up head-butting half the team and ripping the door off his locker," Rollinson said. As a senior, Leinart cemented his legacy at Mater Dei with impressive numbers—more than 2,600 yards and 28 touchdowns—and one particularly memorable performance.

The Monarchs were playing Concord De La Salle, a Northern California school that was on a historic 102-game winning streak. With a crowd of fifteen-thousand watching at Edison Field in Anaheim, they fell behind by three touchdowns in the first quarter before their leader calmly sparked a rally. Time and again, Leinart drove the offense downfield, finding open receivers, converting on fourth downs, throwing for more than 400 yards. In the final moments, he got his team within range of a tying field goal only to watch the kick sail wide left. Although Mater Dei lost 31–28, the crowd roared in appreciation.

Meanwhile, about an hour up the freeway, the Trojans were on the verge of a five-game losing streak that eventually got Hackett fired. Rollinson, who had played a season at USC in the early seventies, recalled telling his quarterback, "It's a new deck of cards," and Leinart started thinking about a visit to Oklahoma. Pete Carroll had some quick talking to do over December and January. It didn't hurt when he kept Pola on the staff and hired Norm Chow—a longtime friend of Steve Clarkson—as offensive coordinator.

A reassured Leinart said he liked the coaches now leading USC. On national signing day in February, he officially took his place in the first recruiting class of the Carroll era.

———

This wasn't like Shaun Cody arriving on campus to great expectations. It wasn't like Mike Williams and LenDale White, who showed up a year later. When Leinart looked at the USC roster in 2001, he could not have seen a great likelihood of starting right away. Sure, he was promised a chance to compete for the job, but Palmer still had an aura, a vestige of that golden image. Leinart figured to spend a year finding his way around campus, getting used to college classes, and learning Chow's system. Then, after Palmer had a fabulous junior season and left school early for the NFL, the new guy could assume the number one spot in 2002.

It seemed like a reasonable enough plan, except it didn't work out that way.

Within months, the Trojans had lurched to a 2–5 start, and there were rumblings, people wondering about a change. Before the game against Arizona, Carroll gathered his offensive coaches for a round-table discussion. Steve Sarkisian recalled, "It was, 'Does this team need a shakeup? Maybe Carson Palmer can't win. He's a great player but . . . maybe we just need a fresh start. Let's put this young kid in and we'll live and die with him for the next four years.'" As a graduate assistant working with the quarterbacks, Sarkisian doubted that Leinart was ready, but the staff decided to work the freshman into the rotation.

Over the next week, Leinart shared repetitions with Palmer in practice and, by his own estimation, was "throwing the ball well. It was the best I had been doing." Carroll apparently agreed. He called Bob Leinart to say that Matt would play the second quarter against Arizona. "I go, 'What?'" Bob recalled. "He goes, 'Well, we're going to play him one quarter, at least, every game the rest of the year.'"

On Friday, Bob and Linda got in the car and began driving to Tucson for their son's college debut. They were on the road when the phone rang again. This time, it was Matt. "I'm not playing," he said. The coaching staff had changed its mind. Bob's first reaction was to turn around and head home but, he said, "We were already halfway to Arizona, so we kept going." The Leinarts sat in the stands on a warm night and watched as Kris Richard returned an interception for a touchdown to give USC a thrilling victory. The win led to a four-game streak and an invitation to the Las Vegas Bowl—and that's where the second part of Leinart's plan fell through. In the aftermath of a frustrating day against Utah, Palmer chose not to apply for early entry into the NFL draft. He was coming back for a final season.

Instead of assuming command of the Trojans offense, Leinart spent the spring and summer of 2002 fighting Matt Cassel for the backup spot. He opened the season at number two on the depth chart, but as Palmer put together a Heisman-winning season, the redshirt freshman struggled to stay motivated. "He was pouting," his father said. "He had a bad attitude." Leinart agreed. "It was tough to just really keep battling for a backup position," he said a few years later. "You have to really stay on top of your game and stay mentally involved. You can't get down on yourself, and when you do get an opportunity, you have to make the best of it. I struggled to do that." Even worse, the coaches now doubted his physical skills. They did not see his arm strength progressing as they thought it should have. Carroll, in particular, was concerned about how he was delivering the ball.

Soon, Cassel was getting more snaps in practice, and the best Leinart could manage was mop-up duty in a few games. Two snaps against Colorado. A few series at Oregon. A single play against UCLA. Not a single pass thrown. At the Orange Bowl, with a victory over Iowa assured, it was Cassel who came in for the final moments. When the game ended, the question of Palmer's successor—already on everyone's mind—was up in the air. Sarkisian, stepping aside from postgame celebrations on the field, said flatly, "Tomorrow, we'll start focusing on what we've got and figure out how to handle it."

During that off-season, Leinart was less than convinced about his chances. He showed up at Rollinson's office one day. The Mater Dei coach had watched the young man's confidence wilt over the previous two seasons and, like the Trojans coaches, had been waiting for him to step up. "Here," he said, handing Leinart a videocassette. "Put on the De La Salle tape. Where's *that* guy?"

————

The criteria for winning the job was simple. The next USC quarterback did not need to be another Palmer. The focus was on efficiency, avoiding turnovers, and taking advantage of opportunities that presented themselves. As Sarkisian said, "We're not going to ask him to go out and win the Heisman Trophy." Heading into spring practice, four guys had a shot.

First there was Cassel, the longtime backup. Over the course of his years at USC, coaches had on several occasions urged the big, athletic player to switch to tight end and, in 2001, he had actually caught a 12-yard pass against California. But the junior insisted on sticking to his original position. "It's been a long time coming," he said. "I paid my dues . . . I'm going in with the mind-set of being the starter and getting this team ready to go." Also in the mix was Brandon Hance, who had been a starter at Purdue before transferring to USC. Six feet tall, he was smaller and quicker than the others. The question was, had he recovered sufficiently from surgery? "If my shoulder heals up the way I'm hoping it will, I think I can be the number one guy," he said. Another backup, Billy Hart, also on the baseball team, was simply hoping to get a look.

And then there was Leinart. Shaggy hair and a wide smile. A blonde surfer-model for a girlfriend. And that questionable arm.

Taking Rollinson's words to heart, Leinart became a fixture in the weight room. "He made up his mind, 'OK, I'm going to work out and get in the best shape of my life. I'm going to give it everything I've got. Let's see what happens,'" his father said. Now 6'5" and 215 pounds, he was also determined to change his attitude. There would be no more pouting like the season before.

More and more, Chow was impressed. "I never worry about arm strength," he said. "It's decision-making. . . . You just knew he was the guy because he was bright." At one point, the offensive coordinator even pulled Bob Leinart aside and predicted that Matt would win the job. Yet, as spring practice unfolded, none of the hopefuls stood out from the crowd, and Carroll remained noncommittal. One day, the head coach said the situation "hasn't taken shape yet to make a declaration." The next day, he suggested that, "If we were playing a football game, Matt Leinart would start." Then he quickly added, "The competition remains open." In a final spring scrimmage at the Coliseum, most of the snaps went to Leinart and Hance, neither of them moving the offense particularly well.

For all the big high school games Leinart had played, all the tough spots in youth baseball, this was difficult territory. Instead of staying relaxed, letting the ball go, he was too careful, too worried about throwing interceptions.

If anything, the situation grew even cloudier because the Trojans were recruiting John David Booty, who many experts considered the best prep quarterback in the nation. After watching two spring workouts, the kid from Evangel Christian Academy in

The Ugly Duckling

Shreveport, Louisiana, walked right into Carroll's office and verbally committed to USC. A month later he announced that he would skip his senior year in high school, graduating early so he could enroll in the fall. Was it a sign that he had been promised a chance to win the starting job?

Leinart tried to stay cool. He praised Booty's decision, saying, "It's a chance for him to come in and get some experience and compete. It would be tough for anyone to come in and learn the system in three weeks, but I know he's a good player." Leinart also said, "You always have to compete, and you can't worry about other guys and what they are doing." The sophomore went back to the weight room and continued to work through summer, adding a few more pounds of muscle.

With the start of training camp in August, his efforts began to pay off. Although the coaches were impressed with Booty—"He has excellent tools. You can't hide it," Carroll said—Leinart made good on Chow's prediction by steadily distancing himself from the pack. He was passing with more zip, less hesitation. As the days went by, Cassel struggled with consistency, Booty with injuries, and Hance appeared weakened by a summer bout of viral meningitis. Two weeks before the season opener, Leinart completed 11 of 15 passes for 190 yards and a touchdown in a scrimmage that Carroll called his best performance as a college quarterback.

"I didn't force anything," Leinart said. "I threw the ball away when I needed to and completed passes when I needed to and kept the offense moving."

If there was any doubt about who would start the season opener against Auburn, it all but evaporated two days later. During drills, Leinart got hurt blocking 285-pound defensive lineman Mike Patterson on a reverse play, his throwing hand bruised and numb. X-rays showed no broken bones, and Carroll sensed an important moment. With the offense practicing goal-line plays a while later, he summoned the injured quarterback from the sideline and said, "Hey Matt, it's a game. Can you go back in?" Leinart did not hesitate, toughing it out through several snaps. "It hurt a little bit, but I went out there to show my teammates," he explained. "You gotta go out there and play hurt or whatever."

Afterward, when asked about naming a starter, Carroll grinned broadly. "We have a starting quarterback," he said. "We have a number one guy."

CHAPTER 12

The Next Step

The trip took an hour or so, north on Interstate 85, across flat Alabama countryside that was just beginning to feel the brunt of the day's heat. Matt Leinart sat on the team bus with a good idea of what awaited him. Not just a game against nationally ranked Auburn. This was his *first* game as a starter, in a hostile stadium, with some very large shoes to fill.

"I'll look around a little bit because it's impossible to ignore," the redshirt sophomore said of his pregame plan. "Then you just block it out. You just have to come back and get focused and play."

Pete Carroll was preaching a similar message to the rest of the USC team. After too many years on the outside, the Trojans had forced their way back into college football's elite with an Orange Bowl victory the previous January. Now, at the start of the 2003 season, they needed to forget all that and rededicate themselves because the bar had been raised. To take the next step, they would have to compete for the national championship—with a brand-new quarterback. "It's about as drastic as you can go," Carroll said.

More than eighty-six thousand orange-clad fans—almost none of them showing Southern hospitality—packed into Jordan-Hare Stadium on that sweltering evening to watch the opener between sixth-ranked Auburn and eighth-ranked USC. If Leinart was concerned about nerves, he did not have to worry for long. His defense quickly intercepted a pass, giving him a short field to work with.

Three plays later, he rolled to his left, calmly waited for receiver Mike Williams to break free, then tossed his first official pass five yards for a touchdown. "After I threw that touchdown pass and completed a few passes on third downs, I realized this was pretty easy compared to practicing against our own defense," he said.

At least one national magazine had picked Auburn to go all the way, a forecast that quickly fell by the wayside. Cadillac Williams, the dangerous running back, spent most of the evening getting run over by new middle linebacker Lofa Tatupu. Meanwhile, quarterback Jason Campbell was constantly scrambling, sacked six times. "A good defensive line can dominate a football game," he said. "That is exactly what happened." Given the luxury of a lead, Leinart remained cautious, putting together only a few more drives. His conservative 192 passing yards paced the Trojans to a 23–0 win.

"He had no turnovers and threw some good balls," said Williams, his loquacious receiver. "I'll give him a 9½."

But one game did not a veteran make. Not at barely 20 years old. A week later, Leinart ran hot and cold against Brigham Young, passing for three touchdowns and suffering as many interceptions in a 35–18 victory that was closer than it should have been. Against an overmatched Hawaii, he was steadier, though his most memorable play was a block thrown for Reggie Bush. Then came the start of the Pacific-10 Conference schedule.

The third-ranked Trojans had a sense of what lay ahead. Four of their next five games would be on the road against tough competition, beginning with a California team that had nearly beaten them the season before. USC arrived early to Memorial Stadium in Berkeley that day—unusual for a squad that usually kept to a tight routine. Players found themselves running around on the field and sitting around in a cramped locker room. Defensive lineman Shaun Cody recalled that Mark Jackson, the director of football operations, said to him, "I don't feel right about this. Something's different."

The game could not have gotten off to a worse start. On the second play, Cal running back Adimchinobe Echemandu ripped off a 36-yard run over right tackle, the start of a big day for him and his offense. While the Golden Bears looked sharp, Leinart was struggling, throwing interceptions on consecutive possessions, forcing his team to come from behind in the second half. The Trojans were down by three points with less than five minutes remaining when they got the ball back with one more chance to win.

Starting at midfield, Leinart connected with Williams on two passes, driving his offense inside the Cal 25-yard line. There was still time to take a few shots at the end zone, yet Carroll and Norm Chow suddenly turned conservative. Were they afraid of their young quarterback making another mistake? Carroll said no, they were simply trying to surprise Cal with some unexpected play-calling. Whatever the reason, the Trojans ran on three consecutive plays and settled for a field goal that sent the game into a wild overtime.

Tailback Hershel Dennis fumbled, but USC survived because 6'8" tight end Gregg Guenther Jr., the tallest player on the team, blocked a Cal field-goal attempt. Both teams scored touchdowns after that. Finally, kicker Ryan Killeen missed a 39-yard attempt and Cal took advantage, making its 38-yard kick for a 34–31 victory in triple-overtime.

"You get to thinking it can never happen," Carroll said. "It can. You can get beat."

The Trojans' 11-game winning streak—stretching over parts of two seasons—had ended, and any hopes for a national championship were in serious jeopardy. Lingering just outside the old stadium, Carroll pondered over a lackluster running game and a shaky, young quarterback. For only the second time in his tenure at

Conquest

USC—the other being that loss to Stanford in the first season—the steadfastly optimistic coach could not hide a look of uncertainty.

———

From the first day of training camp, it had been clear that LenDale White embodied two very important characteristics in a tailback. At 6'2" and 225 pounds, he had the size. Even better, he had the attitude.

"Nasty," was how Carroll described his running style. "That's something we really like."

The freshman was part of an impressive group of young runners at USC in 2003. There were fellow newcomers Reggie Bush, the breakaway artist, and Chauncey Washington. There was also Dennis, the sophomore and anointed starter. But in the days after the Cal loss, Carroll became intent on taking pressure off Leinart by establishing a power ground game. And that put the focus mainly on White.

It was an unlikely scenario if only because the young man had grown up with lukewarm feelings toward football. As a five-year-old, he cringed at the sight of his cousins playing in a Denver youth league. His uncle signed him up the next fall, and every year for three years, White wanted to quit. "My mom and uncle wouldn't let me," he said. As a 14-year-old freshman at Denver South High, he rushed for nearly 200 yards in his first game and helped his team to an 8–3 record. By the end of his sophomore year, he had amassed an astounding 4,270 yards.

Still, he didn't like the game all that much.

His outlook changed, in part, because of a frightening incident in which a man showed up at practice with a gun. Though no shots were fired, White's family transferred him to Chatfield High in suburban Littleton for his junior season. Somehow, the new surroundings triggered something inside him, despite the fact he had to awaken at 5:45 A.M. for the 40-minute drive to his new school. "That's when I started to really love football," White said. "Forty minutes was not going to hold me back from being there at 7:00 A.M. to work out with the rest of the team."

As a junior, White led Chatfield to an undefeated season and a state title. As a senior, he made everyone's prep All-America team and boosted his career rushing total to 7,803 yards, best in state history. With scholarship offers from Texas, Michigan, and Oregon, he chose USC because, like Mike Williams before him, he saw an opportunity to play right away. Justin Fargas, Sultan McCullough, and Malaefou MacKenzie were gone. Dennis was the only returning tailback. "I just knew they would need other people to come in and take reps," White said.

Dennis got the majority of the carries through the first two games of 2003, but, more and more, the Trojans were moving toward a tailback-by-committee. In the third week, against Hawaii, White and Bush offered a glimpse of the future by rushing for two touchdowns each. White followed that with another touchdown at Cal. With each passing day, he became more of a presence. In the locker room, teammates knew him as lively and talkative, always joking. On the field, he was a motivator, pumping his fists, thumping his chest.

As the Trojans prepared for Arizona State, Carroll yearned for that kind of emotion, the sheer intensity that Fargas had supplied the previous season. "We're going to look to see who's hot and go with the guy," Carroll said. "I want to get us flying at the line of scrimmage and see if we can get good push and make things happen a little bit better than we have." White insisted he was ready. "Everybody looks forward to the day when they get a chance to prove who they are and prove what they can do," he said.

His day was about to arrive.

Conquest

———

The quarterback situation continued to weigh heavily on Carroll's mind the week before Arizona State. Not only had Leinart been inconsistent, he was hurting with knee and groin injuries. The coach said, "He gives us the best chance to win right now. We'll stay with him." Hardly an overwhelming vote of confidence. But on a hot October afternoon in Tempe, with the season at a crossroads, the kid did something more than just hold onto his job.

The Trojans were losing in the second quarter at Sun Devil Stadium when Leinart got knocked out of the game by a blitzing linebacker. At halftime, X-rays showed no serious damage to that bruised right knee and, now, a sprained ankle. The question was: could he play through the pain? Chow told Brandon Hance to be ready, but Steve Sarkisian, the quarterbacks coach, went to Leinart and said, "The team needs you." Leinart hobbled out of the locker room early in the third quarter. "Sometimes," he said, "you just have to go out there and play hard and forget about the pain."

It was like that day in training camp when he shook off a hand injury. Leinart completed two consecutive passes, and a few plays later, USC tied the score. The Trojans caught fire, scoring on four of their next five possessions, Leinart doing just enough to transform a tight game into a 37–17 runaway. He got plenty of help from White, the tailback on his way to a bruising 140 yards, making good on Carroll's determination to reestablish the run. The defense pitched in, too, forcing a pair of turnovers. But afterward, everyone was talking about the guy who limped back into the huddle.

"He could have easily packed his bags and got changed," guard Fred Matua told Chris Dufresne of the *Los Angeles Times*. "He knew we needed him. When things were down, he was there." Williams added, "As to the question about who needs to be the quarterback on this team, I hope nobody asks me. I think it's obvious at this point."

The Next Step

The ninth-ranked Trojans were 4–1 and back in the hunt. The next week, Leinart tossed three touchdown passes to Williams in a big win over Stanford. The week after that, he threw for 351 yards and four touchdowns in a landmark victory at Notre Dame. It was only the second time in two decades that USC had won in South Bend, and the final score, 45–14, represented the team's widest margin of victory in a long history of visiting the revered stadium. Former USC quarterback Pat Haden, an analyst for Notre Dame broadcasts, later said that he had never seen receivers so wide open. Leinart concurred, downplaying his hot streak, "I'm just hitting open receivers and making the right decisions."

After beating the Irish, the Trojans climbed into the top 5 in the polls but still were being punished for the loss at Cal, ranking only No. 7 in the bowl championship series standings. That left them on the fringes of the title picture. "I don't care," Carroll said. "We have to go play. At the end is when it counts." On the road against Washington, his team dominated, with Leinart passing for another four touchdowns and Bush amassing 270 all-purpose yards on long pass plays and kick returns. Washington linebacker Marquis Cooper said, "USC is a great team—that's the bottom line."

It remained to be seen if the BCS agreed.

———

His father and grandfather had been high school coaches so, as a boy, Jacob Rogers sat at the table and watched them draw up plays, learning his Xs and Os right along with his ABCs. "I've always been a student of the game," he said. In the fall of 2003, he also ranked among the best offensive tackles in the nation, proof that USC had finally rekindled its proud tradition of elite linemen.

Two seasons earlier, as a sophomore, Rogers had seen considerable action on a unit that had generated a paltry 87.7 rushing yards per game, worst in the conference, and had given up all those sacks. The low point had come in the Las Vegas Bowl against Utah, the Trojans finishing with a miserable one yard on the ground. Rogers was among the returnees who vowed to do better.

The line had been coached by the quiet and unassuming Keith Uperesa. In the spring of 2002, Carroll hired someone to work with him. The new guy, Tim Davis, could not have been more different. He stood a towering 6'7", with a broad forehead and bushy mustache. Much like Ed Orgeron, he cut a larger-than-life figure on the practice field, ceaselessly loud and fiery.

During that first off-season, Davis insisted his linemen report together for 6:00 A.M. workouts. When training camp began, he scrambled from drill to drill. Once, while the players were stretching, he stuck his nose in Matua's face mask and chewed out the lineman for some previous indiscretion. A young boy watching from the sideline turned to his father and said, "Dad, I think I'll stick to baseball." Yet these tough-love tactics and his unrelenting motivational spirit produced a fierce allegiance. "Coach Davis, he can be crazy," Matua said laughing. "But he brings out the best in you."

With Rogers leading the way, and talented freshman Winston Justice playing tackle opposite him, the line showed significant improvement in 2002. By the end of the season, USC had climbed to third place in the conference with an average of 142.5 yards rushing. "I think we're starting anew, starting our own dynasty," Justice said. As the team prepared for its game against Iowa in the Orange Bowl, Carroll informed Uperesa he should seek employment elsewhere.

By 2003 Davis was running the show and the line was better than ever. Norm Katnik had become a solid center. White and Bush, nicknamed "Thunder and Lightning," were running for more and more yards as the season wore on. A once-maligned unit was considered a strength, drawing praise from none other than the legendary former lineman Anthony Muñoz. And Rogers, playing through injury, got much of the credit.

"He's like a coach on the field," Davis said. "He understands the whole game."

With a shaved head and round face, the 6'6", 305-pound Rogers looked like a big kid and was gentle-mannered. Much of his success could be attributed to playing tight end in high school, developing footwork that now helped him stay in front of fleet defensive ends. This agility, and the wisdom that came with growing up as a coach's son, cast him as the leader of the resurgent Trojans line.

"The thing we lacked in years past, that we captured last year, was confidence," he said. "Before, we kind of questioned ourselves here and there. But now we've come together and we really have a tight-knit team. I think this has the makings of something really special."

———

No one wanted to talk about it. Not Carroll. Not any of his players.

The crystal trophy awarded to the winner of the BCS championship was on a tour of college stadiums and scheduled to stop by the Coliseum. But the Trojans, standing fourth in the BCS, were in no mood to think about the title race, all those complicated computer rankings, the mind-numbing formulae. Maybe they were better off when the trophy's visit had to be canceled because of brush fires burning through parts of Southern California. There would be no distraction from the task at hand.

The first week of November brought a showdown with sixth-ranked Washington State at the Coliseum. Days before the game, Cougars defensive lineman Isaac Brown told the *Seattle Times* that USC's defensive front four was overrated. Brown said, "If you want to hold them up to the gold standard, go ahead . . . I think they get a lot of hype because they're USC." He probably should have kept his mouth shut.

Conquest

On a clear, cool Saturday evening, defensive end Kenechi Udeze sacked Washington State quarterback Matt Kegel in the first quarter to start an onslaught. Next came Omar Nazel. Mike Patterson. Shaun Cody. By game's end, the defensive line had seven tackles for losses, including five sacks and a forced fumble. "It was personal," Udeze said. The Cougars' potent offense never had a chance to get started and, on the other side of the ball, Leinart continued his string of big games, passing for three more touchdowns. It all added up to a 43–16 victory.

Now the Trojans stood second in the BCS standings, high enough to qualify for the title game at the Sugar Bowl, and the next few weeks had all the looks of a championship run. First came a shutout victory at Arizona. Then a dominant performance against UCLA that could be summed up by a single play. On the opening drive, Leinart floated a pass down the right sideline to Mike Williams. In one fluid motion, the big receiver leaped high for the ball, made the catch, and slammed 5'9" cornerback Matt Clark into the ground, stepping over his prone body in the end zone. The game was, for all intents and purposes, over.

The Trojans had earned a share of the Pacific-10 championship and, at the very least, their first trip to the Rose Bowl in almost a decade. In any other season, this would have been cause for celebration, but the players had a bigger prize in mind. Although they had slipped to third in the BCS, losses by Miami and Ohio State made it likely they would recapture the all-important second spot. "It's in our hands now," offensive lineman Lenny Vandermade said. "Everything is right there in front of us." One more game remained on the schedule, one more chance to impress the voters.

Oregon State had a good team that season but lacked the firepower to stay with the Trojans. Again, Williams provided a signature moment. Running a short route into the end zone, he appeared to be taken out of the play by an Oregon State safety draped across his back. As the ball whizzed past, he reached out with his left hand and snagged it on his fingertips. "I guess I could have made it with two hands," he said. "I was just trying to have fun, though." USC was on the way to a 52–28 victory.

The Coliseum erupted in a raucous party at the final gun. Keary Colbert waved a box of sugar as fans draped Mardi Gras beads around their necks. The 11–1 Trojans felt certain they had secured a trip to New Orleans to play for the title. In a crowded, exuberant locker room, senior cornerback Marcell Allmond pulled on a T-shirt that read, in gold letters, "Got Sugar?"

———

The offense had made most of the headlines that fall—stories of the gutsy young quarterback, the phenomenal receiver, the freshman tailbacks. But this was still a Pete Carroll team, still founded on defense. And, along the front line, Kenechi Udeze was becoming a star in his own right.

By the end of the regular season, he was leading the team in sacks and on his way to becoming a consensus All-American. Ed Orgeron called him the best defensive end he had ever coached—"by far"—high praise from a man who had overseen the dominant Miami lines in the late eighties and early nineties. Udeze, whose name meant "Thanks be to God" in the Ibo language of Nigeria, spoke of his success as if it were a dream come true.

The 6'4" junior might never have ended up at USC if not for Orgeron's eye for hidden talent. In this case, the talent was hidden under approximately 355 pounds. That was Udeze's weight at Verbum Dei High, where he was a gifted pass rusher who had trouble tying his own shoes. Orgeron saw potential in the big kid—just like he had with Mike Patterson—and told Udeze a scholarship awaited if he could slim down. The offer sparked a transformation. Udeze started working out more and stopped eating late-night pizzas.

"There was a big change," said Arie, his mother. "Food was in the refrigerator . . . not in his mouth."

Even so, he arrived on campus at 300-plus pounds, still befitting the nickname "BKU," as in *Big* Kenechi Udeze. The coaches redshirted him as a freshman, adamant that he get lighter. Sitting in study hall one day, the teenager doodled a comical self-portrait in a notebook. Muscles rippled from the bare-chested, Hulk-like figure, accompanied by outlandish statistics and a quote from television analyst John Madden proclaiming him "the next sure thing." Udeze tacked the drawing on the wall of his dorm room for inspiration. "I've always been a big dreamer," he said.

His weight continued to drop, and he broke into the starting lineup, collecting 7.5 sacks as a sophomore. Eventually, at 280 pounds, he looked as sculpted as that improbable cartoon. And he wasn't exactly shy about taking his shirt off in the weight room.

In the fall of 2003, there was pressure to perform. USC was touting its line—Udeze and Nazel, Cody and Patterson—as the "Wild Bunch II." It was an homage to the original "Wild Bunch," the 1969 unit known for its hard-nosed style of play. As if that weren't motivation enough, during the summer, a USC recruit named Drean Rucker drowned in a swimming accident off Huntington State Beach. The Trojans joined his family for a ceremony near the site, and Udeze was moved. "Even at my house, I still have the booklet from his memorial service on my refrigerator and a little picture of him to keep him in my heart every day," he said. He vowed to dedicate his first tackle of each game to Rucker.

His first big performance came against Stanford, with three sacks, two forced fumbles, and a blocked field goal. Then he had two sacks at Notre Dame and two more on that angry evening against Washington State. In all, he got to the quarterback 13.5 times in the regular season, and the media began speculating that he might skip his senior year to head straight for the pros.

That was something the otherwise talkative Udeze did not want to discuss. The young man who had predicted his future with a drawing on the wall had one more dream to fulfill in college—he wanted to play for a national championship. Only this time, he knew that no amount of discipline or determination, no hours in the weight room, would make a difference. The Trojans could only wait for the final BCS standings.

Carroll walked into the room smiling. That had to mean good news, right?

Less than 24 hours after their victory over Oregon State, the USC players had gathered to learn whether they still held the No. 2 spot in the BCS and would be invited to the title game. It was a complicated scenario. Top-ranked Oklahoma had lost to Kansas State but had a big cushion, maybe enough to stay on top, and No. 3 Louisiana State was charging hard from below. With the BCS set to release its final rankings that Sunday, middle linebacker Lofa Tatupu and his teammates sat anxiously in a meeting room at Heritage Hall. They saw the grin on their coach's face and wondered if it meant they should start packing for New Orleans.

"I was thinking, 'Maybe he's just putting us on,'" Tatupu recalled. "Then he told us we are the No. 1 team in the nation, but . . ."

Both the Associated Press and ESPN/*USA Today* polls had USC in the top spot, but the BCS was a different story. It also included seven computer ratings and, when those numbers were factored into the equation, Oklahoma finished first and LSU second. USC was third by 0.16 of a point. "Does that mean we'll get the crystal football, or won't we?" defensive lineman Frostee Rucker asked his coach. Stunned players filed into an adjacent dining hall to watch the televised announcement. After only a few minutes, Mike Williams walked out, saying, "The fact we're the No. 1 team and we're not playing in that game . . . that speaks for itself."

It wasn't the first time the BCS had excluded an arguably deserving team and, in other instances, coaches had griped to the media. But with Rose Bowl officials on hand—USC would face Michigan in Pasadena—Carroll accepted their invitation, talked about how happy he was, and issued a challenge to his players. The coaches who voted in the ESPN/*USA Today* poll were contractually bound to select the Sugar Bowl winner as their champion. The writers of the AP poll had no such obligation. The Trojans still had a shot at half of the title.

So the USC team that returned to practice that week was resolute. "A lot of people are going to be wondering where is our focus at, or can we still play strong and finish even though we're not in the BCS game," Williams said. "That's something we've got to go out and prove." They would have to prove it against a No. 4 Michigan team that had one of the best defenses in the nation and a typically brawny Big Ten offense.

On New Year's Day, with the Rose Bowl awash in cardinal and gold, a majority of the sellout crowd rooting for USC, Michigan showed its muscle early. Running back Chris Perry gained steady yardage behind a veteran line, and quarterback John Navarre connected on a handful of passes. But then USC cornerback Will Poole snuck into the backfield for a sack, and the drive stalled. When the Wolverines attempted a field goal, Cody burst through the line and got a hand on the ball. The Trojans were on their way.

Leinart wasted no time. Four passes. Four completions. The last one a 25-yard touchdown to Keary Colbert. In the second quarter, a low pass from Navarre bounced off receiver Braylon Edwards' foot and into the arms of Tatupu, whose interception return set up another score. In the third quarter, Colbert—who had played in Williams' shadow all season—fought off a defensive back while making a one-handed catch and sprinted the rest of the way for a 47-yard touchdown. The score was 21–0.

The Wolverines could list any number of ways in which they struggled that afternoon: the secondary kept giving up big plays, special teams stumbled. Yet, almost to a man, the players pointed to the same thing. "Nine sacks," offensive tackle Tony Pape said. "That's just a terrible statistic." Starting with Poole's blitz on the opening drive, Navarre went down under the Trojans rush again and again. "It was really my greatest fear . . . an extremely quick, athletic front four," Michigan coach Lloyd Carr said. "We just could not handle their pressure up front, and I think that was probably the difference in the game."

Michigan finally scored, late in the third quarter, but that only set the stage for another USC highlight. The Trojans came right back and had a second down at the Wolverines' 15-yard line, the ball placed on the left hash mark. Up in the booth, Chow spotted an opportunity to call a play—"trips right, 18 toss, reverse quarterback throwback"—he had used at North Carolina State and added to the USC playbook only a few weeks earlier. Leinart pitched the ball to tailback Hershel Dennis, who headed for the right sideline, then pitched to Williams on a reverse. With the Michigan defense scrambling to change direction, the left-handed receiver suddenly looked to pass.

"I thought it was a sweep, then I thought it was a reverse, then I couldn't believe it when he threw the ball," Michigan defensive tackle Grant Bowman said. "So they had me three times."

Watching the play unfold, Chow had an entirely different reaction. "I saw the ball coming out of Mike's hand and it looked like it was shot out of a cannon," he said. "I thought it was going to be an incomplete pass." Leinart, all alone in the left flat, reached out and made the catch. "I'm not very fast," he said. "But I've got good hands." The image of the quarterback striding into the end zone, ball held overhead, became a symbol for USC's 28–14 victory that day.

"We dominated a great Michigan team," Leinart said after being selected as the game's most valuable player. "We are the best team in the nation."

Three days later, Louisiana State defeated Oklahoma in the Sugar Bowl to win the BCS title. But, by virtue of their performance in the Rose Bowl, the Trojans remained atop the AP poll and won a share of the national championship, their first since 1978.

"There is no doubt about it," Matua said. "USC is back."

CHAPTER 13

Speed and Wiggle

The kid could play tag for hours on end, dodging, spinning, laughing as he eluded his friends. Loved to run. Couldn't sit still. His parents, looking for ways to exhaust some of that energy, put him in youth baseball and karate lessons. Sometime around the fourth grade, he asked if he could play football.

Reggie Bush was slim as a child, almost wiry, and his mother thought, *Oh, he's going to get hurt.* His stepfather eventually signed him up for a Pop Warner league near their home in San Diego but said that "he didn't look like much" beneath a big helmet and shoulder pads. Then came his first game. The best that LaMar and Denise Griffin can recall, their son dodged and spun for almost 300 yards and a handful of touchdowns that day. Later in the season, he had a 500-yard game. "We had no idea," LaMar said. Denise added, "He always had the attitude: 'Why are you guys so surprised?'"

Being good at football made perfect sense to Bush. "I was playing a game I loved," he said. "A game I was supposed to play."

The teenager who enrolled at Helix High in La Mesa had grown up enough to impress coaches with his raw physical talent, running the 100-meter dash in a startling 11.4 seconds. As a freshman. In tennis shoes. Donnie Van Hook, an assistant then, told the other coaches, "This kid is going to be the best player from San Diego since Marcus Allen." About that time, LaMar recalled, a teacher caught Bush fidgeting in class, staring into the distance, ducking his head from side to side. "What are you doing?" the teacher asked. He was envisioning an open-field run, darting through imaginary tacklers.

As a junior, Bush made all-state by rushing for more than 2,200 yards. As a senior, despite missing four games with a broken wrist, he scored 27 touchdowns, was a consensus All-American and ranked among the top high school backs in the nation. But it wasn't only numbers that made him special. All the major college programs came knocking at his door because of a quality that was difficult to put into words. He was so quiet that classmates sometimes mistook him for being arrogant. His coaches and teammates knew better. They knew that every ounce of his boundless energy was funneled into the game.

"He showed his emotions by how he played football," Van Hook said. "What he would do, instead of getting wild, jumping up and down, he would just play harder."

For all the yards that Bush rushed for at Helix—nearly 5,000 over the course of his career—and all the times he carried his team to victory, the performance that sticks in Van Hook's memory was a defeat. It was Bush's final game in high school, an upset loss to rival Oceanside in the championship. Just like when he was a boy—playing all day, coming home, falling into bed—Bush ran for 144 yards and returned a kickoff 91 yards for a touchdown before collapsing because of cramps in the fourth quarter. His parents were there to drive him home but, slumped in the locker room with an intravenous needle sticking in his arm, he pleaded with his coaches, "Please hold the team bus. I want to go home with my teammates."

"For being that good, he was a pretty humble kid," Van Hook said. "A definitive team player."

Bush insists he was only doing what came naturally. His mother recalled a day when she was watching the evangelist T. D. Jakes on television while her son finished his homework in the dining room.

Jakes was talking about having a purpose in life. Bush suddenly pushed away from the table and walked into the living room.

"Mom, that's what I feel like," he said. "I've been anointed to play football."

———

The Griffins lived in a modest townhouse just off the freeway, family photographs adorning a living room that was kept tidy. It was never the sort of home where a youngster—even a prodigiously talented youngster—could get a swelled head. Denise worked as a deputy sheriff in the county jail, a job that suited her sense of decorum. "My parents were so strict," she explained. "You had to say 'Yes, sir' and 'Yes, ma'am.' You did not talk back." When Bush was still a toddler, she married LaMar, a school security officer and church minister who had similar ideas about raising kids. God always came first and the boys—they have a younger son named Jovan—always followed the rules.

"Not too strict, but they stayed on top of us," Bush said. "I had to do my homework and clean my room. Chores every weekend."

If his sons left the house without making their beds, LaMar hustled outside and made them come back. When it became clear that Bush was unusually talented at football, treated as special by other kids and parents, LaMar sat the young man down for a talk. "You have to make a decision in your life," he said. "You want to set yourself apart? You've got to do it the right way." That meant staying humble and working hard in practice, never stepping foot on the field unless he intended to give his all. It also meant helping opponents up after a tackle, patting them on the helmet and, most of all, staying out of trouble off the field. Because of their jobs, his parents knew something about kids who got in trouble. "We talked a lot," Bush said. "They were always reminding me."

By the fall of 2002, a rare combination of skill and attitude had Bush rated among the most sought-after recruits in the nation. Everyone knew that he wanted to play for Tyrone Willingham, the new coach at Notre Dame. Washington and Texas were also on his list of candidates. And what about the Trojans? As Ed Orgeron, the recruiting coordinator said, "We didn't think we had a chance." Then they got some unexpected help.

LaMar had prayed over the matter and told his son it might be a good idea if they drove north on Interstate 5 a couple of hours to have a look. The USC coaches hastily arranged a visit. Alex Holmes, the personable tight end, played his customary role as tour guide, showing Bush around campus before taking him to dinner with quarterback Matt Leinart and receiver Mike Williams. Even more impressive to Bush was practice. Watching from the sideline, he liked the upbeat tempo, the way guys flew around the field.

In the weeks that followed, his parents could see that he was struggling to decide. Bush traveled to San Antonio to play in the prestigious U.S. Army All-American Bowl, a nationally televised game that featured all of the best high school players. He kept calling home, starting to tell them something, then stopping short. "Slowly," he said, "my mind was changing." Among the elite recruits invited to Texas, it had become fashionable to announce their decisions during the game. LaMar watched on television as his son spoke with a sideline reporter.

"He said he was going to USC," the stepfather recalled. "My phone started ringing. Pete Carroll called. Lots of other people. It was crazy."

———

Speed and wiggle.

That was how Carroll described his new tailback after the first day of training camp in 2003. "Really cool," he said. The coach went back to his office and called a buddy in the NFL, asking for a copy of an old Chicago Bears' highlight reel. He wanted Bush to see how the legendary Gale Sayers ran with the ball, the way Sayers turned on a dime, his speed and fluidity. "I just wanted to throw that out there for Reggie," Carroll said.

The first time the freshman lined up against the first- and second-team defenses in full pads, he broke into the secondary for one long gain after another. Catching a short pass out of the backfield, he reversed direction and sprinted 30 yards for a touchdown, drawing cheers from his teammates. Bush downplayed his performance, saying he still had a lot to learn, but as offensive lineman Norm Katnik would later marvel, "When you see Reggie back there, you know it's going to be a different type of running."

It wasn't long before fans got a taste of this explosiveness. In the third game of the season, against Hawaii, they chanted his name from the stands after he sprinted for touchdowns of 23 and 27 yards. Then came a dazzling cutback and 58-yard score at Notre Dame, showing the Irish what they had missed. Then the 270 all-purpose yards at Washington. "I didn't know he was that good," Husky defensive end Terry Johnson said. Against Oregon State, Bush caught two more touchdown passes.

"I've never seen a guy come out of high school like [him]," said Dirk Koetter, the coach at Arizona State. "He's fantastic."

Even Carroll, who saw Bush in practice every day, found himself continually amazed. Watching the new tailback sail through opposing defenses a dozen times that season, the coach sounded like a fan. "It's so fun to know when he's gone," Carroll said. "You get to enjoy the end of the play." Seemingly the only thing that could slow Bush was the crowd in his own backfield. That fall, the Trojans had an embarrassment of riches, talented sophomore Hershel Dennis as the designated starter, rotating with Bush and the other newcomer, LenDale White. Carroll was particularly fond of the way his three backs complemented each other. Dennis was all finesse, setting the stage for the Thunder and Lightning freshmen—the powerful White and the electric Bush.

Sharing the ball was not quite as enjoyable for the players themselves. "It's a little tough for a running back to get into a rhythm when you're not in there getting all the reps and feeling the defense," Bush mused. Ultimately, they had no choice but to adjust. "We had to be friends," White said. "If we weren't, it would never have worked out." Their camaraderie was born of equal parts respect and competition. The freshmen, champing at the bit, spent the first minutes of each game watching Dennis. Whenever one of them made a big play, the others wanted to match it. All the while, Carroll looked for signs of discontent, listened for hints of grumbling. "They seem so fresh and young, they're just fired up to be part of the team," he said. "They don't even think that way."

It helped that the Trojans were winning and, besides, there was enough action to go around. Although Bush finished third on the team in rushing for 2003, he had 1,331 all-purpose yards, led the Pacific-10 in kickoff returns, and made freshman All-American. Better yet, USC averaged 155.9 yards a game on the ground. Bill Doba, the Washington State coach, said the Trojans were "back to Tailback U."

———

The young man who was becoming a star at USC still had a hint of boyishness in him. Although he had grown to be 6' tall and 200 pounds, his upper body woven with threads of muscle, he remained trim and compact in appearance. His precise face seemed almost elfin. And, for all his flamboyance as a runner, Bush proved downright shy in most other ways.

There were rarely signs of emotion during games—no pumping of fists or, as his high school coach put it, getting wild. Around strangers, he was unfailingly polite and soft-spoken. When reporters asked about one of his runs after a game, he often tried to deflect credit to his teammates. "He's flashy in how he plays, not a flashy guy," Leinart said. Running backs coach Todd McNair, who spent eight years in the NFL, would later suspect that Bush did not quite grasp his growing celebrity.

"It's kind of sneaking up on him," McNair said. "He still doesn't realize who he is."

LaMar and Denise recalled that after each road game, their son would call on his cellphone and, no matter how many yards he had gained or how many touchdowns he had scored, would ask the same unassuming question. "How'd I do?" His fame was creeping up on them, too. Walking out of the Coliseum one Saturday afternoon, they were approached by a fan who blurted out something along the lines of, "Your son is God." Denise thought, *Don't put my boy on that kind of pedestal.* It went against everything they believed. Her husband said it out loud.

"No," LaMar told the fan. "He's not God."

Yet there was no denying Bush could perform at an extraordinary level, if not an utterly different speed. Sometimes when he got the ball, gliding those first few steps, sizing things up, the stadium would hold its breath. What was coming next? A spin move or razor-sharp cutback? Maybe a burst of acceleration that would leave defenders standing in their tracks. "It feels like all the pressure is lifted off my shoulders," was how he described it. "I'm just running and, when I'm all by myself, it's a sense of relief." Despite his parents' insistence on humility, Bush succumbed to occasional flourishes—showboating, even—launching himself into the air as he crossed the goal line. The first time came against Hawaii, punctuating a 27-yard score. He mentioned something about a defensive back racing at him from the side, then relented. Well, yes, maybe the dive had been merely for show.

Conquest

After the Trojans won a share of the 2003 national championship, they were invited to the White House where President George W. Bush commented on sharing a last name with USC's explosive tailback. Around the locker room, Reggie was already known as "the President," a joke that paid subtle homage to his growing stature both on the team and throughout college football. There was something else about the seemingly modest kid, an extravagant side that the more-vocal White revealed.

"Reggie's a shopaholic . . . tennis shoes, clothes," White said after a game. "Top model of the year."

Jeans, caps, and dozens of sneakers—every last pair kept as clean and crisp as the day they left the mall—filled the closet in Bush's apartment. The guy who could be so whirlwind-quick on the field was exasperatingly slow when it came to getting ready, unwilling to step foot out the door until everything looked just right. Hair, clothes, everything. His friends complained that he was always making them late. They nagged him to cut down on his primping, but he settled upon a different solution, "I'll just start getting ready earlier."

The only two people who seemed to understand were his mother—she had been something of a shopper in her youth—and his voluble teammate. "Quiet but flashy," White said. "If Reggie doesn't look good, he doesn't feel like Reggie."

———

Despite all the roles that Bush had played for USC during the 2003 season, there was a sense that he had barely scratched the surface. During the spring, Chow visited the St. Louis Rams to take notes on how they used Marshall Faulk in their offense. He and Carroll were eager to experiment with their sophomore.

They wanted to add punt returns to his repertoire. Also, with Keary Colbert gone to the pros and Mike Williams considering an early entry in the NFL draft, they needed to use Bush as a receiver more often, both in the slot and out wide. "We'll just try to keep increasing the amount of little things he can do within those roles," Carroll said. "It's nothing he can't handle." During a scrimmage at the Coliseum in March, Bush scored on a 14-yard run, turned a short pass from Leinart into a 60-yard touchdown play, and strung together several impressive returns. He said simply, "You just want to go out there and put on a show for the crowd."

Then came an incident during summer camp that put even more of an onus on the versatile young back.

In mid-August, the Los Angeles Police Department announced that it was conducting a sexual assault investigation involving one or more USC players. According to documents subsequently released by the district attorney, a young woman claimed she had visited an off-campus apartment where a number of players were staying. She told authorities that alcohol and marijuana were present and that she had nonconsensual sex with one of the players. Within days, Carroll suspended Hershel Dennis for violating unspecified team rules. Law enforcement sources confirmed Dennis was at the focus of their investigation.

The woman eventually recanted her allegation, telling prosecutors that no force was used and that she had not objected to the sexual intercourse, the documents said. No one was arrested and no charges were filed. But by then, the investigation had stretched into fall. Dennis, who was reinstated after nearly a month, said, "I felt like I really let my teammates down . . . by bringing all this bad publicity about USC. Coach Carroll always says to stay away from situations that can hurt the team. Then a mistake like this happens, and I feel bad about it."

Back in August, Bush was shaken by what was happening. It went back to his upbringing, all those parental admonitions about being careful. "You just have to recognize who you're with and, if there's trouble, you have to get out of there," he said. There were on-the-field concerns, too.

The Trojans were preparing for their opener against Virginia Tech—a tough opponent on the road—and with Dennis suspended at that point, sophomores Bush and White would have to carry the load. Bush, already being touted as one of the most exciting players in college football, said, "We're up for the challenge. We can't look ahead, but we know what's out there."

CHAPTER 14

"No Doubt"

Twenty-two hundred miles to the east, a running back named Maurice Clarett had been suspended from the Ohio State team and wanted to turn professional. Clarett was only a sophomore, too young for the NFL rule that said no player could be eligible for the draft until three years past his high school graduation, so he sued. On February 5, 2004, a federal judge in New York ruled that the league's age limit violated antitrust laws. At which point all eyes shifted to USC and Mike Williams.

Williams had just finished an All-American sophomore season in which he had toyed with opposing cornerbacks. Those hands and that 6'5" frame. A straight-for-the-jugular mentality. Not to mention 95 catches and 16 touchdowns. Of all the underclassmen in college football, he seemed among the most capable of jumping to the next level.

At first, Williams downplayed suggestions of his leaving. Asked about the Clarett decision, he said, "Maybe it will open the door for others who think they can succeed, but I always thought the rule was fine the way it was. So this ruling has nothing to do with me." Within days, however, word leaked that the 20-year-old was reconsidering, which started a minor panic in and around the program. Even with the backfield triumvirate of Matt Leinart, Reggie Bush, and LenDale White returning, USC's hopes of repeating as national champions rested heavily on the star receiver. As Norm Chow later explained, "You're talking about a great athlete."

The next seven months played out like a bad soap opera, starting with Pete Carroll's efforts to coax Williams into staying. Rumors spread that the player was faring poorly in the classroom. In an interview with the campus newspaper, the *Daily Trojan*, he criticized teammates, questioning their commitment. That led to a flurry of meetings, players discussing the problem among themselves, Carroll summoning Williams to his office. On February 25, Williams told reporters that he was turning pro.

"I just felt like I was going to take my opportunity through a door that was opened by someone else," he said.

Not only did he make the announcement, he signed with an agent which made him instantly professional—and thus ineligible—in the eyes of the NCAA. It was a risky maneuver if only because the Clarett case was still under appeal. Sure enough, in April, an appellate court blocked the lower court's decision, and the Supreme Court subsequently declined to consider emergency appeals by Clarett. Williams was in limbo, banned from playing in either college or the pros. When draft day arrived that same month, his agent, Mike Azzarelli, sent him to an island resort so the young man would not have to watch the NFL pass him by.

"It was depressing for me," Azzarelli said. "I can imagine it would have been for him too."

By early June, Williams was attempting a reverse every bit as complicated as the trick play that had scored a touchdown in the Rose Bowl. Cutting all professional ties with his agent, he enrolled in summer classes at USC and, with help from the school, filed for reinstatement. Initially, Williams said, the NCAA demanded that he pay back any money he had received and earn passing grades in his classes. As the days went by, however, officials kept asking for more and more information. In public, Williams said, "It makes me feel like they're making a fair evaluation." Privately, however, Chow said the young man grew increasingly pessimistic. When training camp began—the Trojans were ranked No. 1 in the preseason polls—Williams attended practices for only about a week before agreeing with Carroll that he should sit out until a decision came down.

To some degree, the coaching staff was resigned to proceeding without him. "There isn't enough time to deal with that stuff," Chow said. "You have to move on." But the team was finding that success came with a price. The months before camp had brought the usual defections, assistants leaving for other jobs, defensive end Kenechi Udeze leaving for the pros. Then came unexpected losses. Winston Justice, the offensive tackle, was arrested for flashing a replica gun in a parking lot and then suspended for two semesters. Tight end Dominique Byrd broke his kneecap playing basketball with, of all people, Williams. Another receiver, Whitney Lewis, did not make grades. Finally, midway through training camp, tailback Hershel Dennis came under investigation for sexual assault and was suspended indefinitely for violating team rules.

So, approaching the season opener against Virginia Tech, the Trojans still held out hope for Williams' return. The athletic department kept a seat open for him on the team plane, but as the players were preparing to leave for the game in Landover, Maryland, Carroll received a call on his cellphone. For 10 minutes, he paced back and forth on the practice field, listening intently, his expression increasingly dour. The NCAA had denied reinstatement.

Williams appeared to take the decision calmly, as if the summer of turmoil had spoiled his taste for playing. "I'm kind of done with it, I guess," he said. Chow later said that the receiver was actually quite upset. Carroll made no attempt to hide his feelings. "To take it all the way to one hour before we leave?" he said of the NCAA ruling. "I couldn't be more disappointed. It's very cold and insensitive of them to deny him this opportunity."

With that, he climbed on the team bus, heading for Los Angeles International Airport and the start of the 2004 season.

———

In years past, whenever things got rough, the team could count on the emotional Omar Nazel or Melvin Simmons to speak up. Now, those guys were gone, and the USC locker room was silent. Players sat in front of their stalls, no one saying a word. Lofa Tatupu, the middle linebacker, recalled, "You could hear a pin drop."

The Trojans had traveled to Landover, Maryland, with a No. 1 ranking and dreams of back-to-back national titles but quickly ran into harsh realities. First, they were informed that Williams would not be joining them. Second, when game day came around, they played a Virginia Tech team that exposed their weaknesses. The USC receivers? They struggled to get open and dropped passes. The defensive line? Without Nazel and Udeze, Virginia Tech quarterback Bryan Randall was running free. By halftime, the Hokies had taken a 10–7 lead and their legion of fans—by far the majority of the sold-out crowd—had transformed FedEx Field into one long, deafening roar.

All of which led to a quiet USC locker room at halftime. A couple of players eventually spoke up, albeit briefly, before the coaches emerged from their meeting. On this night, the Trojans would have to rely on something other than emotion. Carroll gave his defense some adjustments to deal with Randall while, on the other side of the ball, the offense pretty much turned things over to Reggie Bush.

The versatile tailback had scored USC's only touchdown on a screen pass in the first quarter and sensed that more would be required of him in the second half. He got his chance after a controversial penalty. Officials called Virginia Tech for offensive interference on a pass play that would have put the Hokies in scoring position. Instead, USC got the ball back. Lining up wide left, Bush dashed through the secondary and caught a 53-yard touchdown pass from Leinart. After a Virginia Tech field goal, he started in the backfield and drew a mismatch against a linebacker, scoring on a 29-yard reception. "I always feel like I'm going to take over the game . . . it's just a matter of getting the ball in my hands," he said. The defense held Randall to minus-14 yards in the final 30 minutes, and USC held on for a 24–13 victory.

There were two ways to look at what happened that night. Certainly the Trojans had defeated a tough team in what was essentially a road game. Yet so many doubts persisted, even through victories over outmanned Colorado State and Brigham Young in the following weeks. The receivers, sophomore Steve Smith and freshman Dwayne Jarrett, who acknowledged having "jitters" early on, needed to grow up fast. There were concerns about the defensive line and the secondary, where several key players remained untested. If the Trojans were going to make it to the national championship game at the Orange Bowl, they needed to find some answers. And quick.

The final weekend of September took them to Stanford for what should have been a comfortable win. Except the first half was a disaster. Stanford scored with conventional pass plays and a fake field goal. With seconds remaining before halftime, Cardinal running back J. R. Lemon took a handoff and ducked into the line as if to run out the clock. No one tackled him. He dashed 82 yards for yet another touchdown to make the score 28–17. Leinart said, "It was kind of a dagger."

Once again, the USC players found themselves in a bad situation, in a strange locker room. Only this time, it would not be so quiet. Before anyone realized what was happening, the defensive and offensive lines were standing face to face. Slowly, other players closed in like kids expecting a schoolyard fight. The first words came from offensive guard John Drake.

"What are you going to *really* do about them running the ball?"

Defensive tackle Shaun Cody answered, "What are you going to do about keeping Matt Leinart off the ground?"

The verbal challenges shot back and forth, growing louder each time. Then a funny thing happened. The players started yelling *with* each other instead of *at* each other.

"We're going to take over this game," Drake bellowed.

"Right here," Cody answered. "Right now."

Pretty soon, the boisterous LenDale White joined in. So did the usually quiet Bush and Leinart. Teammates were bouncing off each other and knocking over water coolers. "It was the most fun, the most intense situation I've ever been in," Tatupu said. Finally, from out of nowhere, Carroll stepped in.

"All right! All right!" the coach yelled. "I know you guys are excited. Listen up. We've got some checks to go over."

This wasn't a Hollywood movie. The Trojans did not come charging out to score 50 consecutive points. But the defense held Stanford scoreless, and the offense found ways to reach the end zone, Bush with a spectacular punt return to set up the winning touchdown. USC escaped, 31–28. "Every team looks for a chance to define what they are going to be about," Drake said of the halftime scene. "Right there, at that moment, we figured out what we were going to be about."

———

Maybe the only guy who didn't yell in that locker room at Stanford that day was Matt Grootegoed. Speaking up had never been his forte. Then again, Grootegoed never needed to make noise to get noticed.

The senior was part of a trio—along with defensive linemen Shaun Cody and Mike Patterson—that formed the cornerstone of the USC reclamation project. "We built this program around them," defensive line coach Ed Orgeron said. "They helped turn this thing around." While Cody and Patterson had based their careers on obvious physical talents, Grootegoed had come by his success in another way.

"No Doubt"

A star on defense and offense at Mater Dei High—also alternating at quarterback with Leinart for part of one season—Grootegoed originally came to USC as a safety under Paul Hackett. Then Carroll showed up and was, to say the least, unimpressed. "He didn't make any plays," the new coach said. "He just looked like a nothing guy out there." So Carroll spliced together a videotape of "lowlights" and called Grootegoed into his office for a bit of in-your-face career assessment. There was a method to this madness. Instead of burying the kid down the depth chart, Carroll wanted him to switch positions. Grootegoed, scratching his head at the mention of that day, recalled, "There wasn't anybody at linebacker, so I figured I could try out for that."

It seemed like a long shot. He was neither big enough, at 205 pounds, nor familiar with the nuances of the position. Yet "the closer he got to the football, everything started happening for him," said Nick Holt, the linebackers coach at the time. Grootegoed moved right into the starting lineup by making the most of his natural assets. He had a nose for the ball and quickness for pass coverage. Against the run, this young man who was so reticent around strangers, rarely speaking above a murmur, never flinched when taking on larger opponents.

"I've never seen a guy like him," Tatupu said. "Sometimes you look at him and wonder how he does it."

If anything, Grootegoed's ferocity could work against him. His first season at linebacker, in 2001, was cut short by a broken leg against California. In 2003 he struggled with a high ankle sprain, his numbers suffering. But in between, in 2002, he stayed healthy enough to put together a breakout performance, leading the team in tackles and sacks and making the all-conference squad.

Now, the fall of 2004 was starting even better. His name popped up on several preseason All-American lists, and his teammates voted him defensive cocaptain. Carroll had switched him to the weak side, which meant he did not have to wrestle with big tight ends anymore. Grootegoed responded with six tackles in the opener against Virginia Tech, two interceptions against Colorado State and another against BYU, and seven tackles at Stanford.

No one around the team—or around the nation, for that matter—thought of him as small anymore. Ken Norton Jr., a USC assistant and former all-pro linebacker, explained, "Pound for pound, he's the baddest guy on the team."

———

With less than two minutes remaining on the clock, the math was brutally simple. USC had a six-point lead. California had first and goal at the 9. The next few plays would decide the game.

Tatupu looked around the huddle and saw his teammates barely hanging on. Cody. Patterson. Grootegoed. All of them looked exhausted. But Tatupu saw something else. "The hate in their eyes," the middle linebacker said. He told them, "You couldn't have a better ending. Especially with what happened to us last year."

The Trojans had lost in triple overtime to Cal the previous season, a defeat that had cost them a clean shot at the national title. Now, with a 4–0 record and a No. 1 ranking, they were back in the same fix. After opening an early lead, they had watched the seventh-ranked Golden Bears fight back thanks to quarterback Aaron Rodgers, who had tied an NCAA record by completing his first 23 passes in a row. *Wow, is he ever going to miss?* USC linebacker Dallas Sartz wondered.

"We dominated the game," Rodgers said. "We drove up and down the field."

The Golden Bears also squandered opportunities, fumbling in scoring position and missing a short field goal. With time running out and the score 23–17, Rodgers had one last chance, scrambling

and connecting on three passes to help move his team within spit-
ting distance of the end zone. There was 1:47 remaining, and, as
USC defensive tackle Manuel Wright said, "It was scary serious."

As desperate as the situation might have seemed for the Trojans,
secondary coach Greg Burns saw reason for hope. Most of Rodgers'
completions that day had come on short passes, underneath the coverage. This close to the goal line, not much territory left to defend,
the USC cornerbacks could tighten down. And the crowd at the
closed end of the sold-out Coliseum was producing a roar unlike anything heard in the stadium for decades. If only the Trojans players
could hold up. "We were running on empty," Cody said.

On first down, Rodgers threw a pass that was too low for receiver
Noah Smith to get his hands on. USC cornerback Justin Wyatt
breathed a sigh of relief, saying, "Thank God." On second down,
Rodgers started to dish a shovel pass to running back J. J. Arrington,
but had to pull back because Arrington got lost in a muddle of
linemen. That split-second hesitation gave Wright a chance to break
through. Rodgers scrambled to the right with the big man on his
heels. "I thought he was going to outrun me, but I was pulling
closer," Wright said. "I thought, *I'm going to have to leap to grab him.*"
The quarterback went down for a five-yard loss, making it third and
goal from the 14.

The fans were so loud that the Coliseum was shaking as USC
called a timeout and Carroll gathered his defense on the sideline. Just
like that day in 1991 when his New York Jets mounted a goal-line
stand against the New England Patriots, the coach found himself in a
surprisingly upbeat mood. No yelling or finger-waving. These kinds
of situations were tailor-made for a man preternaturally drawn to
competition. "As good as it gets," he told his guys. "The perfect
setting."

The Trojans got one step closer to victory when, on third down,
Rodgers barely missed on a pass that sailed through the end zone.

Conquest

With Cal down to its last chance, defensive end Frostee Rucker wanted to tell his teammates that this time would be different, this time they would not lose to the Golden Bears. He tried yelling to them but recalled, "You couldn't hear anything anyway."

With the USC defensive players waving their arms, urging the fans to get even louder, Rodgers took the snap and was forced to his left by the rush. He spotted receiver Jonathan Makonnen working an outside-in move against cornerback Kevin Arbet. "He was trying to get under me for a post," Arbet said. "We got tangled up." The players jostled, and Makonnen slipped to the turf as the pass whizzed just beyond his reach. When the ball hit the ground, Arbet said, "It's over."

————

The first time Lee Webb got a close look at the USC campus he was 12. He had spent the night on a bus-stop bench and was pushing a shopping cart filled with his belongings up Figueroa Street. For a kid living on the streets, the university looked like another world, the trees and grass and stately brick buildings.

"One day," he said out loud. "I'm going to go here."

So it did not really matter that—some 10 years later—hardly anyone noticed the starting fullback for USC. Let Reggie Bush and LenDale White grab all the headlines. Webb was entirely content doing the dirty work, charging through the hole ahead of the tailbacks, taking on linebackers and safeties. When his teammates called him "our backbone," they were talking about more than football.

Webb was only five when his father moved him and his two brothers to Detroit. Their mother promised to come along but did not show up at the bus station. When they returned to Southern California several years later, she was supposed to take them in. That also fell through. They lived on the streets for a while, pushing that

174

shopping cart past USC, then got a place of their own for as long as the money lasted. By then, Webb said, his father had been struggling with a substance abuse problem for some time. The teenager soon bounced between group and foster homes.

Through junior high school, a kind of surrogate family grew up around him. There was Joseph Toliva, the owner of a local car restoration shop who paid Webb to do odd jobs and helped him to stay in school and away from gangs. And Geraldine Turner, a foster parent to one of Webb's friends. She eventually took him in, becoming his legal guardian. And there was football.

Webb first played the game when he was in Detroit and found that, on the field, his troubles faded. "I really could block them out because I loved football so much," he recalled. "Nothing else really mattered." The sport eventually led him to Robert Garrett, the coach at Crenshaw High in South Los Angeles. As Webb became a star running back and linebacker at the school, good enough to attract scholarship offers from across the country, Garrett exhorted him to stay in line and keep his grades up. Maybe the coach sensed that this hard-luck kid had one shot at making it to college.

"Unless you do something drastic right now," Garrett told him, "you don't have a chance."

Soon Webb's grades rose high enough to qualify him for university, and he was studying for entrance exams. In the spring of 2000, on a day that he called "a dream come true," the teenager signed a letter of intent to attend USC. He would never be a star for the Trojans, switching from fullback to linebacker and back again, but in 2004 he was starting almost every game. "He is a big factor on this team," Carroll said. "The kids love him and respect the heck out of him." Even better, the fifth-year senior was on schedule to receive a degree in public policy and management from the school he had dreamed about so long ago. "It's hard to believe," he said. "I pinch myself sometimes."

Conquest

———

No one thought much of it at the time. Back in May, Notre Dame had been looking at the upcoming season and wanted to switch its game against BYU to an earlier date. The change would require USC to postpone its visit to Provo by a couple of weeks. The schools got together and agreed.

Now, in mid-October, it was becoming clear that USC had ended up with a perfect scenario for a championship run. The schedule was arranged around three byes, one after the tough Virginia Tech game, another after the near-upset at Stanford, and a third near the end of the season. The players and coaches could use the off-time to heal and address any problems in practice. The receivers, in particular, seemed to benefit, improving as the weeks went by. "It just seems like it worked out just right," Carroll said.

After the emotional goal-line stand against Cal, the team got another break with a stretch of comfortable victories. Arizona State, Washington, and Washington State—all of them fell by wide margins. Leinart was playing well, as were Bush and White. Steve Smith was out with a broken leg, but the freshman, Dwayne Jarrett, had become a go-to guy. The Trojans were on a roll when they traveled to Oregon State in early November.

Despite USC's traditional domination of the Beavers, Corvallis had been a difficult place to play over the years. There was a famous upset—a muddy 3–0 loss—that spoiled an undefeated season for John McKay back in 1967. More recently, the defeat in 2000 had started USC on a downward spiral and doomed Paul Hackett. This time, the team bus rolled into town and hit a thick fog that enshrouded Reser Stadium. While his players worried about the visibility, Carroll sensed that the Beavers were primed to pull an upset. "You could feel it," he said. "That's what was in the air."

"No Doubt"

From the outset, USC looked tentative. Bush lost a punt in the mists and fumbled. Oregon State kicked an early field goal off that mistake and soon widened the lead to 13–0. Even the USC assistants struggled—up in the booth, they could not tell which Oregon State players were coming in and out of the game. "We were playing in a cloud," Carroll said. It took a couple of spectacular plays to finally clear things up.

With a bit more than four minutes remaining in the half, Leinart threw a pass in the general direction of Dominique Byrd. The big tight end caught sight of the ball but had a defender draped over him. "I just threw an arm up there," he said. His one-handed touchdown catch brought the Trojans back within range. That gave Bush a chance to atone for his earlier turnover with a decisive play in the fourth quarter. It was a trademark moment for the sophomore tailback, fielding a punt cleanly at his 35-yard line and making several quick moves to set up the defense. Then came a sharp cut across the field and a burst of speed. Sixty-five yards later, he was in the end zone, and his team was on the way to a 28–20 win.

"That was kind of a back-breaker," Oregon State receiver Mike Hass said of the punt return. "That guy is incredible."

For the fourth time in a little more than two months, the Trojans had barely escaped an upset, raising questions about how good they really were. Bush offered a different take: championship teams find a way. A 49–9 victory over outmanned Arizona at the Coliseum the next week improved the Trojans' record to 10–0. With only two regular-season games remaining, they were tantalizingly close to an undefeated season and an invitation to the BCS championship game at the Orange Bowl.

First came another of those crucial byes, a chance for injured players such as Steve Smith and offensive lineman John Drake to rejoin the lineup, a chance for everyone to regroup. As it turned out, they would need it.

Conquest

———

Matt Leinart enjoyed the spotlight at first, but after a while the media crush began to overwhelm him. The photo shoots. One interview after another. It was getting to be too much. And this was two weeks *before* the start of the season.

All spring and summer—ever since he caught that touchdown pass from Mike Williams in the Rose Bowl—he had been in demand. His picture had appeared on the covers of more than a dozen preseason magazines. During training camp, he answered questions from newspaper reporters, moved from camera to camera for the television crews, then laid down on the turf at Howard Jones Field, a cellphone pressed to his ear, doing radio interviews. Finally, in a meeting with offensive coordinator Norm Chow, he broke down.

"It just got to the point where I just was like, 'I have to focus on football,'" Leinart said. "I realize I'm going to have to do a lot of stuff—it's just the nature of the position I'm in. But . . . I don't want to be the only guy on this team getting singled out."

It was almost a relief when the games began, even if it meant having to live up to the expectations that came with being the quarterback for the top-ranked team in the nation. "I'm just going to go out and play the way I know how to play," he said before the opener against Virginia Tech. "Hopefully, that will be good enough."

As the weeks went by, Leinart found that he was being measured in two ways. First, he had to win games, no easy task with a young receiving corps and a left elbow that would remain tender all season from lingering tendonitis. On a separate scorecard, fans and the media were keeping track of his status as a Heisman Trophy contender. One week he was down, eclipsed by Cal's Aaron Rodgers with that record stretch of completions. The next week he was back in the running, throwing four touchdown passes against Arizona State.

"No Doubt"

Through the next four games, he had nine touchdowns with only two interceptions, Carroll seeming almost ho-hum about it, saying Leinart "had another terrific night for us." The quarterback could not pretend to ignore the hype swirling around him. "It's cool, but it's something I can't focus on right now," he said in late October. "I'm aware of the Heisman and being a top candidate, and now that I had a good game last week, people jumped back on the bandwagon . . . but I don't care."

As the Trojans began preparations for Notre Dame, Chow made another prediction to Bob Leinart. Eighteen months earlier, the offensive coordinator had said that Matt was going to win the starting job. This time, he guessed that—just as Carson Palmer had in 2002—Matt was going to shine against the Irish on national television and clinch the trophy.

Leinart came through, passing for a career-best five touchdowns and 400 yards in a 41–10 victory. "He's leading the best team in the country," Chow told reporters. "I think that says something." Bush, who was also garnering Heisman consideration, agreed, "There's not much a defense is going to be able to do to stop him because he's on fire, he's seeing his reads, he's slowing down the game. He's a great player. He's my pick for the Heisman."

———

One more game remained. After getting past Notre Dame, the Trojans needed only a victory over UCLA—a team they had dominated in recent years—to finish off a perfect season and secure a trip to Miami. But with the start of practices that week, Carroll sensed something amiss. He kept challenging his players and still they seemed distracted.

"We were screwed up," the coach said. "We were not mentally right."

Conquest

As the team gathered for its usual Friday meeting in an auditorium at Heritage Hall, Carroll faced a quandary. He did not want to be too angry or look like he was panicking. At the same time, he could not let things stand. There was too much at stake. So he cleared the room of support staff and ordered the doors shut. "Tell me the truth," he said. "What do you really think of [UCLA]?" LenDale White stood up and said, "They're garbage." Bush didn't think much of them either. It seemed that too few of Carroll's players were taking the game seriously. "He was pissed," linebacker Lofa Tatupu recalled. Carroll lit into them. The next day at the Rose Bowl, the coach's fears proved well-founded.

The Trojans jumped to an early lead thanks to a pair of dazzling touchdown runs by Bush, but never developed a rhythm. As a result, they spent the rest of the afternoon relying on Ryan Killeen's five field goals. That allowed the underdog Bruins to hang around. They scored on a punt return and might have tied the game in the second quarter, scooping up a fumble with a clear shot at the end zone, if an official had not blown the play dead. Late in the fourth quarter, quarterback Drew Olson guided his team on a touchdown drive that cut USC's lead to 29–24. There was 2:20 left—just enough time for a wild ending.

The Bruins tried an onside kick, and Matt Cassel recovered, the perennial reserve quarterback saying, "It was probably the biggest play of my career." Three plays later, Bush fumbled back to UCLA. The Trojans defense then intercepted an Olson pass, but as safety Jason Leach tried to run it back, he got stripped. The ball was on the ground, and veteran cornerback Kevin Arbet got there first, showing the good sense to simply fall on it.

No matter how ugly the victory might have been, USC fans showered the field with oranges as the Trojans celebrated their first perfect regular season since 1972. "I'm ready to fly to the Orange Bowl right now," said Bush, who had saved his team with 204 yards rushing and those two touchdowns. There was not much suspense the next day as players again gathered in their dining hall on campus to watch the final BCS standings announced. It was No. 1 USC versus No. 2 Oklahoma. Shaun Cody said, "It's a matchup that's just been waiting to happen."

A week later, the Heisman Trophy ceremony in New York might as well have been a promotion for the game. Leinart and Bush were there as finalists along with quarterback Jason White and running back Adrian Peterson from Oklahoma. Carson Palmer had given Leinart some last-minute advice about how to act: *Go in with the mind-set that you're not going to win. Don't get your hopes up.*

There was no need to worry. The once chubby, cross-eyed kid from Orange County was announced as the 70th Heisman winner. Peterson and White finished second and third. Bush was fifth behind Utah quarterback Alex Smith, who had been his teammate back at Helix High in La Mesa. Leinart stood onstage in a pinstriped suit and blue tie, that hair combed but still fashionably ragged around the edges. He recalled what Palmer had said about his heart beating out of his chest and said, "I think mine is about to do the same thing."

Before long, however, he was talking about going home, putting the trophy away, getting back to practice. "We still have a big, important game left," he said.

CHAPTER 15

The Coronation

The team had stretched and finished with warm-ups. Pete Carroll had played his customary game of catch with an assistant. Everything was proceeding as usual. Until now.

With the big game finally at hand—No. 1 USC versus No. 2 Oklahoma in the Orange Bowl—the Trojans found themselves sitting in a locker room, deep within Pro Player Stadium, for the better part of 15 minutes. Out on the field, so brightly painted in oranges and reds that night, pregame ceremonies were dragging on with officials making announcements and honoring past players. Carroll did not like the idea of waiting. It was like that day back in 2003 when he got his players to the stadium in Berkeley too early. They had come out flat and been upset by California, their only loss that season. Never again had the Trojans varied from their strict pregame routine. They weren't about to do it tonight.

"OK," the coach yelled. "Let's get everybody out."

His players dutifully shuffled through the door to a concrete hallway, standing there for only a moment or so before assistants herded them right back inside. What was going on? The pregame routine was starting all over, the two voluble line coaches, Ed Orgeron and Tim Davis, hollering as they usually did after warm-ups. "We took the guys back and just faked it," Carroll said. "We always want to come out really pumped up."

Conquest

A little after 8:00 P.M., the Trojans finally streamed out of the tunnel in their cardinal-and-gold home jerseys, greeted by a thunderous cheer from the contingent of USC fans in the sold-out stadium. The players pressed together near the end zone, a mass of bodies hopping in rhythm, fists in the air. And, like so many games that season, the top-ranked team in the nation got off to a shaky start.

The Trojans received the opening kick on a gorgeous night for football, not too warm, not too humid. They made good yardage on their first play from scrimmage, a pass to Reggie Bush, who was starting for the injured LenDale White. After that, the offense went nowhere and had to punt. Oklahoma, taking possession on its own 8-yard line, quickly established a plan of attack. Five times in the first six plays, the Sooners sent their prodigious freshman running back Adrian Peterson into the line. His gains were modest, barely enough for a first down, but they helped open up the secondary. Quarterback Jason White completed two medium-range throws, then passed 32 yards to Mark Bradley, who broke free when USC cornerback Eric Wright slipped. Oklahoma had first-and-goal at the 7.

It was exactly as the experts had predicted for this BCS national championship. While the teams appeared almost identical on paper—matching Heisman Trophy quarterbacks, dangerous runners, tough defenses—prevailing wisdom had Oklahoma coming out on top. In a television booth constructed beside the field, network analysts had repeated this prediction and, later, color commentator Bob Griese had told a national audience that Leinart "does not have a supporting cast. He has to play well. The pressure is on Matt Leinart. If he doesn't play well, they don't have much of a chance to win." Sure enough, in those first few minutes, the Sooners looked bigger and quicker. Their offense, led by a veteran line considered the best in the nation, appeared unstoppable.

On second and goal, Jason White threw into double coverage, and receiver Travis Wilson snagged the ball from between two USC defensive backs. Sooners fans were in a frenzy. The Orange Bowl was like a second home to them—this was the team's 18th appearance in the annual game—and they were accustomed to winning in Miami. Their team had taken a 7–0 lead in convincing fashion, marching 92 yards in 12 plays.

Man, defensive end Lawrence Jackson thought, *is it going to be like this all night?* Then, as the defense was coming off the field, lineman Frostee Rucker looked up at the giant video screen and saw a replay of the touchdown. There was a shot of Carroll on the sideline. The coach was laughing.

———

Trips and stumbles. Missed assignments. The Trojans had been through rough starts before. As linebacker Matt Grootegoed said, "We figured it was going to be a close game. There was no panicking." The manner in which they approached the first quarter of this and every other game was a direct reflection of their coach's personality.

Early on, Carroll had learned the value of staying cool. There was one game in particular, back in the fall of 1979, when he was coaching defensive backs at Ohio State. The Buckeyes had struggled on defense and fallen behind Minnesota. Carroll rushed into the locker room at halftime, telling the offensive assistants, "You guys are on your own! You guys are on your own! We can't stop 'em!" Earle Bruce, the head coach then, laughed at the memory of it. "I'll never forget that," he said.

The Buckeyes made a few adjustments and clamped down against the pass, coming back to win 21–17. They would, in fact, go undefeated the rest of the season until losing to USC in the Rose Bowl. The lesson Carroll learned that day was subsequently reinforced during his tenure with the Minnesota Vikings and legendary coach Bud Grant, who did not believe in getting too emotional.

"If you don't have anything to say," he told Carroll, "don't say it." The important thing was to watch and listen and be prepared to fix the game plan at halftime. It was a skill that Carroll developed slowly but surely. "Some of it is inherent because of the way he studies and appreciates the game," said Ronnie Lott, who played safety for him with the New York Jets. "Some of it is seeing so many offenses along the way."

So the coach who arrived at USC in the winter of 2000 believed in patience. Players say the indoctrination began even as they were being recruited. Over and over, through spring practice and summer workouts, through training camp and into the season, they heard the same message: *You can't win games in the first quarter. You can't win games in the second quarter. You win in the fourth quarter.* Even the coaches heard it. "That's what Pete always said," offensive coordinator Norm Chow recalled.

This philosophy had served them well during the 2004 season. While their tendency to start slowly might have driven fans to distraction—and might have sent another type of coach off the edge—it was no problem for Carroll. He walked into the locker room at halftime and talked with his defensive players, asked them what they had seen out there, even asked for their opinions about what to change. Then he formulated his plan. He almost seemed to enjoy the challenge of coming from behind, the adrenaline rush of it. After his team had scored a tense victory over Virginia Tech in the opener, the coach was downright giddy, "Don't you love games like that?" Against Stanford, when a horrid second quarter resulted in an 11-point deficit, he chose to stand aside while his players gave fiery speeches. Later, he said, "My guys refused to lose, and I'm pretty excited to see that."

It was a far cry from the young Ohio State assistant who had rushed into the locker room in a dither. As Bruce suggested, "Obviously, Pete's got some things figured out now."

The Coronation

The Trojans' composure would be tested again in the 2005 Orange Bowl. Trailing by a touchdown in the biggest game of the year—maybe the biggest game in a decade—USC ignored those raucous Sooner fans and simply went about its business. The defense decided to run a few more stunts, Grootegoed said. Maybe a couple of blitzes. Mostly, the linebacker explained, "We just kept playing." And what had Carroll been laughing about after Oklahoma's long scoring drive? He was thinking back to the last time his team had played in the Orange Bowl, when Iowa returned the opening kickoff for a touchdown.

"At least this time," Carroll said, "we made them work for it."

———

Defense wasn't the only issue for the Trojans at that point. From his booth high above the field, Chow felt a hint of urgency regarding the offense. "It was important that we respond," he said. "You don't want things getting out of hand."

In the days before the game, the offensive coordinator had taken his quarterback aside on several occasions. Chow had watched Matt Leinart grow from an uncertain underclassman into a self-possessed leader and he knew the best way to inspire Leinart was to challenge him directly, keep telling him that everything—a perfect season, a national championship, everything—rested on his shoulders. "We're going to ride you this whole game," Chow said.

"You can't do that with just anybody," he explained later. "But you have to realize what that young man was all about."

It did not take long for Leinart to respond. After Oklahoma's touchdown, he completed four consecutive passes to move the ball into Sooner territory, then he came to the line and noticed that tight end Dominique Byrd was being covered by a linebacker. "Really, in our eyes, that's a mismatch," he said. "Dominique is like a receiver."

Taking a short drop, Leinart floated a throw into the night air. That gave Byrd a chance to run under the ball, spin around, stretch out his right arm, and come down with a one-handed catch in the end zone. The score was tied, 7–7, and Chow thought, *We're fine.*

For the next several minutes, the game settled down, neither team doing much. Just before the end of the quarter, USC's Tom Malone punted toward the corner of the field. At first, returner Mark Bradley let the ball drop, watching it roll toward the end zone. Then, with a swarm of Trojans closing in, he inexplicably reached down to pick it up. "Just a boneheaded mistake," he said. Bradley was hit and fumbled. USC recovered at the Oklahoma 6-yard line as Bob Stoops, the Sooners coach, watched dumbfounded. "I have no idea why Mark would have done that," he said. "I was as shocked as everybody in the stadium . . . it's as bad a play as there is." USC tailback LenDale White came into the game with his sore and heavily taped ankle and scored a touchdown. That quickly, the floodgates opened.

There would be no more room for Oklahoma's Peterson to run. The Trojans defense shut him down, dominating the line of scrimmage, forcing the Sooners out of their patient game plan. Twice in the second quarter, Jason White threw into coverage, and both passes were intercepted. "It was stupid on my part, and I should have just thrown it away," he said. Leinart, on the other hand, was hitting his stride. He made good on the first of White's turnovers by throwing a 54-yard touchdown pass to freshman Dwayne Jarrett. On the second, he found Steve Smith in the end zone from five yards out. The so-called "Best Bowl Game Ever" had gone from a tie score to 28–7 in a little more than six minutes. As Oklahoma receiver Mark Clayton said, "It seemed like everything just kind of fell apart."

Watching from above, Chow was having the kind of night that coaches live for. He would send a play down to the field and see it unfold, thinking, *There's the open receiver,* just as Leinart threw to the man. "It was unbelievable," he said. "Matt just knew what was going to be open." All the linemen made their blocks, all the tailbacks hit their holes, and even the plays that shouldn't have worked, somehow did. Late in the second quarter, Leinart threw a deep pass into the end zone where Smith was being tackled by a hapless Oklahoma defender. As he fell, the receiver reached out with a free hand and cradled the ball into his body.

"Almost too easy," Leinart recalled. "It was strange."

By halftime, the score was 38–10, and the game was, by all accounts, over. "When you turn the ball over four times in the first half, you make it pretty difficult to win," Stoops said. "Then, if you allow people to get behind, you . . . give up some big plays . . . the second quarter really pretty much took us out of it."

There were bound to be changes. It happens with any winning program. After the Orange Bowl, Ed Orgeron left to become head coach at Mississippi, and redshirt junior Lofa Tatupu decided to jump to the NFL. Next to go, everyone assumed, would be Matt Leinart.

The Heisman Trophy winner figured to be a first-round pick and instant millionaire in the upcoming pro draft. On a Friday afternoon in mid-January, hundreds of fans gathered in and around Heritage Hall to hear the announcement—then broke into unrestrained cheers when Leinart said he was staying for his final season. "The one thing I realized is that the NFL is a business," he said. "In college, I'm playing for passion and for love of this game. . . . This is fun. There's nothing like this right here. There's nothing like being at USC, winning national championships and being part of this whole program."

More good news followed. On signing day in early February, the Trojans received commitments from Mission Viejo High quarterback

Mark Sanchez and receiver Patrick Turner of Tennessee, among the highest-rated players in the nation. The recruiting class also included three defensive linemen, four linebackers, and three defensive backs, fresh bodies for a unit that was losing key seniors. Allen Wallace, publisher of *SuperPrep* magazine, called the recruits "an amazing group of athletes." But not everything went the Trojans' way. Leinart had elbow surgery in late January. Then the program got hit by a thunderbolt—Chow announced that he was leaving to become offensive coordinator for the Tennessee Titans. His departure revived speculation about a rift with Carroll. Did egos get in the way? Was it Xs and Os, a difference in football philosophy?

At first glance, the rumors were easily dismissed. Carroll and Chow had always remained amicable in public, and everyone knew that Chow had considered other jobs, pursuing a head coaching vacancy at Stanford only months earlier. A jump to the NFL certainly made financial sense, the Titans offering an annual salary of approximately $900,000. Yet, on numerous occasions, Chow had denied interest in the pros. And anyone close to the USC program, anyone who had been on the practice field or in the hallways of the athletic department, sensed tension beneath the surface.

The men were so divergent in personality, one boisterous and dynamic, the other preferring to go about his duties quietly, almost in private. Even as they became one of the most successful coaching duos in college football history, their working relationship had steadily changed. Not only had Carroll assumed more control of the offense, he had given increasing responsibilities to Lane Kiffin, the up-and-coming assistant who also happened to be the son of an old colleague, Monte Kiffin. After the Orange Bowl victory, it was no secret that Carroll was considering further adjustments, maybe another promotion for Kiffin, maybe bringing former quarterbacks coach Steve Sarkisian back from the NFL. Somewhere in the shuffle, Chow faced the possibility of losing some of his play-calling responsibilities.

The Coronation

No one doubted that Carroll would hesitate with such bold moves. Two years earlier, wanting to make Tim Davis the sole coach of the offensive line, he had told Keith Uperesa to look for another job— even as the team was in Miami preparing for Iowa in the Orange Bowl. Just before the 2003 season, wanting to give heralded but struggling freshman Whitney Lewis the No. 4 jersey that he had worn in high school, Carroll took it from veteran quarterback Brandon Hance.

Whatever transpired between Carroll and Chow, it stayed between them. Carroll had only praise for his departing coordinator, and Chow, asked about rumors of friction at a news conference in Nashville, replied, "No, all of that is exaggerated. I owe a lot to Pete Carroll." The only emotional words came from Matt Leinart and his father, who refused to point a finger at anyone in particular but were obviously upset. "It's very disheartening, and I know Matt is also very disheartened," Bob Leinart told *Los Angeles Times* columnist Bill Plaschke. He added, "We know this is a business, but this is the bad part of the business. There's no loyalty, and that's sad."

There were additional losses, the animated Davis joining the Miami Dolphins and quarterbacks coach Carl Smith going to the Jacksonville Jaguars. None of it seemed to faze Carroll, who had talked about change weeks earlier, on that morning after the Orange Bowl. "We expect our people to move on," he said. Still bleary from celebrating till all hours, he was already thinking about the next season, about filling gaps, getting his team ready for another run at the national championship.

"The long process and the long haul begins again," he said, adding, "We live this."

Players leaving, players staying, coaches taking new jobs—none of it mattered on that night at the Orange Bowl. The Trojans were too busy making one-handed catches and leaping to intercept passes, turning a highly anticipated matchup into something more like a coronation.

Any thoughts of an Oklahoma comeback were dashed minutes into the second half when Leinart threw a 50-yard bomb to Smith, setting up a short touchdown that widened the lead to 45–10. After that, a change started to come over the Sooners. "You could see the frustration on their faces," Tatupu said. "You could hear a couple of guys yelling back and talking to each other . . . you started to see them break down." Leinart took the opportunity to do "a little chatting" with Oklahoma defensive end Larry Birdine, who weeks earlier had labeled the quarterback as overrated.

By game's end, Leinart had answered that charge—as well as any suggestions of a Heisman jinx—by throwing for 332 yards and an Orange Bowl–record five touchdowns. Seven of his completions went to Smith, who had 113 yards and three scores. And LenDale White, whose ankle had been a subject of so much concern all week, ran as strongly as ever for 118 yards. His second touchdown of the game, with less than 10 minutes remaining, put the finishing touches on what would be a 55–19 blowout.

"It was really that kind of night for us, a fantastic night," said Carroll, who the day before had hinted to his players that they were primed for a breakout performance. "It all happened exactly as we pictured it."

The defense had never played better, all but shutting down the second-best team in the nation, leaving the Sooners in a daze. Jason White, who had stayed in school for another shot at the title, walked off the field frustrated by his three interceptions. Peterson struggled to explain why he had managed only 82 yards. Stoops knew why, saying, "We just got whipped."

After the final gun, a portable stage was dragged onto the field, and the Trojans were given a giant bowl filled with oranges. Leinart grabbed a few and tossed them into the crowd. Next came the BCS national championship trophy, the one that USC had been denied the previous season. LenDale White plucked the crystal football off its tall black pedestal and held it aloft. Tatupu grabbed it and kissed it. Then everyone scattered to various parts of the field, some players running to see family at the edge of the stands, others hugging their coaches. A few simply wandered around, big smiles on their faces. Up in the ABC booth, Griese had told his audience, "There's no question in my mind that USC is the best team in the nation."

It was past midnight when the players and coaches finally got back to their beach hotel, but it wasn't too late for Carroll to deliver one more challenge. All season long, he had demanded more. More effort in the weight room, more hustle in practice, more concentration in meetings. This request would be different. "No one goes to sleep," he said. "Not until the sun comes up." In a hotel ballroom, food was served and drinks flowed from an open bar. Families were invited and everyone danced to music played by a deejay, Carroll stepping up to the turntables at one point to spin a few songs. "Kind of like a surreal experience," said Jackson, the defensive lineman. The coach offered another description, calling it "Mardi Gras right there at the Diplomat."

They were celebrating something more than a 13–0 record and a national title. This was about a coach getting another chance. It was about Carson Palmer finally living up to his potential and Matt Leinart growing into a leader. Guys such as Alex Holmes and Grootegoed, veterans of the Hackett era, still could not believe the change that had come over their team. Shaun Cody, who had signed with USC when there was no tangible reason to believe things would get better, called it "a wild ride." Maybe the best description came from Leinart. He was pondering the 2004 season but might have been describing the entire turnaround when he talked about "a lot of question marks, and just battling through tough times, a lot of tough games where we could have thrown in the towel."

On that night in Miami, USC had recaptured its place atop the college football world, and Carroll wasn't going to let the sun rise on another day without his guys savoring the victory. "I'm in the middle of something really special," he said. The Trojans had been on a journey that no one could have predicted. An amazing four seasons.

Season-by-Season Results

2001 (6-6)

Sept. 1 **USC 21, San Jose State 10** **Los Angeles**

| San Jose State | 0 | 3 | 0 | 7 | 10 |
| USC | 7 | 7 | 0 | 7 | 21 |

Sept. 8 **Kansas State 10, USC 6** **Los Angeles**

| Kansas State | 3 | 7 | 0 | 0 | 10 |
| USC | 0 | 0 | 6 | 0 | 6 |

Sept. 22 **Oregon 24, USC 22** **Eugene, Ore.**

| USC | 3 | 3 | 7 | 9 | 22 |
| Oregon | 7 | 7 | 7 | 3 | 24 |

Sept. 29 **Stanford 21, USC 16** **Los Angeles**

| Stanford | 7 | 14 | 0 | 0 | 21 |
| USC | 0 | 0 | 10 | 6 | 16 |

Oct. 6 **Washington 27, USC 24** **Seattle**

| USC | 0 | 14 | 3 | 7 | 24 |
| Washington | 7 | 0 | 7 | 13 | 27 |

Conquest

Oct. 13　　　　**USC 48, Arizona State 17**　　　　**Los Angeles**

Arizona State	3	7	7	0	17
USC	0	21	14	13	48

Oct. 20　　　　**Notre Dame 27, USC 16**　　　　**South Bend, Ind.**

USC	7	6	3	0	16
Notre Dame	3	7	7	10	27

Oct. 27　　　　**USC 41, Arizona 34**　　　　**Tucson, Ariz.**

USC	3	28	0	10	41
Arizona	10	3	14	7	34

Nov. 3　　　　**USC 16, Oregon State 13 (OT)**　　　　**Los Angeles**

Oregon State	0	3	7	0	3	13
USC	7	0	3	0	6	16

Nov. 10　　　　**USC 55, California 14**　　　　**Berkeley, Calif.**

USC	7	21	10	17	55
California	7	0	7	0	14

Nov. 17　　　　**USC 27, UCLA 0**　　　　**Los Angeles**

UCLA	0	0	0	0	0
USC	14	3	7	3	27

Las Vegas Bowl

Dec. 25　　　　**Utah 10, USC 6**　　　　**Las Vegas**

Utah	7	3	0	0	10
USC	0	0	6	0	6

2002 (11-2)

Sept. 2   **USC 24, Auburn 17**   Los Angeles

| Auburn | 7 | 7 | 0 | 3 | 17 |
| USC | 7 | 7 | 3 | 7 | 24 |

Sept. 14   **USC 40, Colorado 3**   Boulder, Colo.

| USC | 14 | 6 | 0 | 20 | 40 |
| Colorado | 0 | 0 | 3 | 0 | 3 |

Sept. 21   **Kansas State 27, USC 20**   Manhattan, Kan.

| USC | 0 | 6 | 0 | 14 | 20 |
| Kansas State | 0 | 12 | 7 | 8 | 27 |

Sept. 28   **USC 22, Oregon State 0**   Los Angeles

| Oregon State | 0 | 0 | 0 | 0 | 0 |
| USC | 0 | 13 | 6 | 3 | 22 |

Oct. 5   **Washington State 30, USC 27 (OT)**   Pullman, Wash.

| USC | 7 | 0 | 7 | 13 | 0 | 27 |
| Washington State | 10 | 0 | 7 | 10 | 3 | 30 |

Oct. 12   **USC 30, California 28**   Los Angeles

| California | 14 | 7 | 0 | 7 | 28 |
| USC | 3 | 14 | 7 | 6 | 30 |

Oct. 19   **USC 41, Washington 21**   Los Angeles

| Washington | 7 | 0 | 0 | 14 | 21 |
| USC | 7 | 10 | 17 | 7 | 41 |

Oct. 26	USC 44, Oregon 33				Eugene, Ore.
USC	14	0	20	10	44
Oregon	13	6	0	14	33

Nov. 9	USC 49, Stanford 17				Palo Alto, Calif.
USC	14	7	14	14	49
Stanford	7	3	0	7	17

Nov. 16	USC 34, Arizona State 13				Los Angeles
Arizona State	3	7	3	0	13
USC	10	10	0	14	34

Nov. 23	USC 52, UCLA 21				Pasadena, Calif.
USC	21	7	14	10	52
UCLA	0	7	0	14	21

Nov. 30	USC 44, Notre Dame 13				Los Angeles
Notre Dame	6	7	0	0	13
USC	0	17	13	14	44

Orange Bowl

Jan. 2, 2003	USC 38, Iowa 17				Miami
Iowa	10	0	0	7	17
USC	7	3	14	14	38

2003 (12-1)

Aug. 30	USC 23, Auburn 0				Auburn, Ala.
USC	10	0	6	7	23
Auburn	0	0	0	0	0

Season-by-Season Results

Sept. 6   **USC 35, Brigham Young 18**   **Los Angeles**

| Brigham Young | 0 | 5 | 7 | 6 | 18 |
| USC | 21 | 0 | 0 | 14 | 35 |

Sept. 13   **USC 61, Hawaii 32**   **Los Angeles**

| Hawaii | 3 | 3 | 7 | 19 | 32 |
| USC | 3 | 28 | 21 | 9 | 61 |

Sept. 27   **California 34, USC 31 (3OT)**   **Berkeley, Calif.**

| USC | 7 | 0 | 14 | 3 | 7 | 31 |
| California | 7 | 14 | 0 | 3 | 10 | 34 |

Oct. 4   **USC 37, Arizona State 17**   **Tempe, Ariz.**

| USC | 7 | 3 | 14 | 13 | 37 |
| Arizona State | 7 | 3 | 7 | 0 | 17 |

Oct. 11   **USC 44, Stanford 21**   **Los Angeles**

| Stanford | 0 | 14 | 0 | 7 | 21 |
| USC | 13 | 28 | 0 | 3 | 44 |

Oct. 18   **USC 45, Notre Dame 14**   **South Bend, Ind.**

| USC | 21 | 7 | 10 | 7 | 45 |
| Notre Dame | 14 | 0 | 0 | 0 | 14 |

Oct. 25   **USC 43, Washington 23**   **Seattle**

| USC | 14 | 6 | 9 | 14 | 43 |
| Washington | 7 | 7 | 3 | 6 | 23 |

Nov. 1   **USC 43, Washington State 16**   **Los Angeles**

| Washington State | 0 | 10 | 0 | 6 | 16 |
| USC | 3 | 12 | 14 | 14 | 43 |

Conquest

Nov. 15	USC 45, Arizona 0					Tucson, Ariz.
USC	14	21	10	0	45	
Arizona	0	0	0	0	0	

Nov. 22	USC 47, UCLA 22					Los Angeles
UCLA	0	2	7	13	22	
USC	14	19	14	0	47	

Dec. 6	USC 52, Oregon State 28					Los Angeles
Oregon State	7	7	7	7	28	
USC	14	14	21	3	52	

Rose Bowl

Jan. 1, 2004	USC 28, Michigan 14					Pasadena, Calif.
USC	7	7	14	0	28	
Michigan	0	0	7	7	14	

2004 (13-0)

Aug. 28	USC 24, Virginia Tech 13					Landover, Md.
Virginia Tech	3	7	0	3	13	
USC	7	0	7	10	24	

Sept. 11	USC 49, Colorado State 0					Los Angeles
Colorado State	0	0	0	0	0	
USC	7	21	14	7	49	

Sept. 18	USC 42, Brigham Young 10					Provo, Utah
USC	0	21	0	21	42	
BYU	0	3	7	0	10	

Season-by-Season Results

Sept. 25	USC 31, Stanford 28				Palo Alto, Calif.
USC	10	7	7	7	31
Stanford	7	21	0	0	28

Oct. 9	USC 23, California 17				Los Angeles
California	0	10	7	0	17
USC	10	6	7	0	23

Oct. 16	USC 45, Arizona State 7				Los Angeles
Arizona State	0	7	0	0	7
USC	14	28	0	3	45

Oct. 23	USC 38, Washington 0				Los Angeles
Washington	0	0	0	0	0
USC	0	10	21	7	38

Oct. 30	USC 42, Washington State 12				Pullman, Wash.
USC	21	14	7	0	42
Washington State	0	0	12	0	12

Nov. 6	USC 28, Oregon State 20				Corvallis, Ore.
USC	0	7	7	14	28
Oregon State	6	7	0	7	20

Nov. 13	USC 49, Arizona 9				Los Angeles
Arizona	3	0	6	0	9
USC	0	14	21	14	49

Nov. 27	USC 41, Notre Dame 10				Los Angeles
Notre Dame	7	3	0	0	10
USC	3	14	10	14	41

Conquest

Dec. 4	**USC 29, UCLA 24**				Pasadena, Calif.
USC	10	10	3	6	29
UCLA	0	10	7	7	24

Orange Bowl

Jan. 4, 2005	**USC 55, Oklahoma 19**				Miami
Oklahoma	7	3	0	9	19
USC	14	24	10	7	55

USC Coaching Staffs

2001

Pete Carroll	Head coach/Defensive coordinator
Norm Chow	Offensive coordinator/Quarterbacks
Nick Holt	Linebackers
Lane Kiffin	Tight ends
Wayne Moses	Running backs
Ed Orgeron	Defensive line/Recruiting coordinator
Kennedy Pola	Special teams
Keith Uperesa	Offensive line
DeWayne Walker	Associate head coach/Secondary
Kirby Wilson	Wide receivers
Steve Sarkisian	Offensive graduate assistant
Rocky Seto	Defensive graduate assistant
Chris Carlisle	Strength and conditioning
Mark Jackson	Director of football operations

2002

Pete Carroll	Head coach/Defensive coordinator
Greg Burns	Secondary
Norm Chow	Offensive coordinator
Tim Davis	Offensive line (guards and centers)
Nick Holt	Linebackers
Lane Kiffin	Wide receivers

Ed Orgeron	Defensive line/Recruiting coordinator
Kennedy Pola	Running backs/Special teams coordinator
Steve Sarkisian	Quarterbacks
Keith Uperesa	Offensive line (tackles)/Tight ends
Brennan Carroll	Offensive graduate assistant/Special teams
Rocky Seto	Defensive graduate assistant/Safeties
Chris Carlisle	Strength and conditioning
Mark Jackson	Director of football operations

2003

Pete Carroll	Head coach/Defensive coordinator
Greg Burns	Secondary
Norm Chow	Offensive coordinator
Tim Davis	Offensive line
Nick Holt	Linebackers
Lane Kiffin	Wide receivers
Ed Orgeron	Assistant head coach/Defensive line/ Recruiting coordinator
Kennedy Pola	Running backs/Special teams coordinator
Steve Sarkisian	Quarterbacks
Rocky Seto	Safeties
Brennan Carroll	Offensive graduate assistant/Tight ends
Dennis Slutak	Special teams graduate assistant
Chris Carlisle	Strength and conditioning
Mark Jackson	Director of football operations

2004

Pete Carroll	Head coach/Defensive coordinator
Greg Burns	Secondary
Brennan Carroll	Tight ends
Norm Chow	Offensive coordinator
Tim Davis	Offensive line

USC Coaching Staffs

Lane Kiffin	Wide receivers/Passing game coordinator
Todd McNair	Running backs
Ed Orgeron	Assistant head coach/Defensive line/ Recruiting coordinator
Rocky Seto	Linebackers
Carl Smith	Quarterbacks
Ken Norton Jr.	Defensive graduate assistant/Linebackers
Dennis Slutak	Special teams graduate assistant
Chris Carlisle	Strength and conditioning
Mark Jackson	Director of football operations

All-Americans and Heisman Winners

All-Americans

2001

Troy Polamalu, safety

2002

Carson Palmer, quarterback
Troy Polamalu, safety

2003

Matt Leinart, quarterback
Tom Malone, punter
Jacob Rogers, offensive tackle
Kenechi Udeze, defensive tackle
Mike Williams, receiver

2004

Reggie Bush, tailback
Shaun Cody, defensive lineman
Matt Grootegoed, linebacker
Matt Leinart, quarterback

Mike Patterson, defensive lineman
Lofa Tatupu, linebacker

Heisman Trophy Winners

2002
Carson Palmer, quarterback

2004
Matt Leinart, quarterback

Depth Charts

2001 DEPTH CHART
Offense

SE	2	Kareem Kelly (6'0", 190) Jr.
	82	D. Hale (6'1", 185) So.*
LT	77	Jacob Rogers (6'6", 290) So.*
	67	Phillip Eaves (6'6", 315) Jr.*
LG	62	Norm Katnik (6'4", 275) So.*
	75	Faaesea Mailo (6'3", 325) Sr.
C	78	Lenny Vandermade (6'3", 275) So.*
	62	Norm Katnik (6'4", 275) So.*
RG	69	Zach Wilson (6'5", 300) Jr.*
	76	Joe McGuire (6'5", 300) Fr.*
RT	66	Eric Torres (6'5", 305) So.*
	71	Nate Steinbacher (6'5", 300) So.*
TE	19	Kori Dickerson (6'4", 235) Sr.*
	81	Alex Holmes (6'2", 275) So.

* = used redshirt season

Conquest

QB	3	Carson Palmer (6'5", 220) Jr.*
	10	Matt Cassel (6'5", 220) Fr.*

FB	28	Charlie Landrigan (5'11", 235) Sr.*
	34	Chad Pierson (6'0", 245) Jr.*

TB	4	Sultan McCullough (6'0", 195) Jr.*
	39	Sunny Byrd (6'0", 220) Jr.*

FL	83	Keary Colbert (6'1", 195) So.
	17	Devin Pitts (6'4", 190) So.

Defense

DE	94	Kenechi Udeze (6'3", 295) Fr.*
	56	Omar Nazel (6'5", 235) So.*

NT	90	Ryan Nielsen (6'5", 280) Sr.*
	99	Mike Patterson (6'2", 285) Fr.

DT	84	Shaun Cody (6'5", 255) Fr.
	90	Ryan Nielsen (6'5", 280) Sr.*

DE	25	Lonnie Ford (6'3", 260) Sr.*
	91	Bobby DeMars (6'4", 250) Sr.*

SLB	59	Chris Prosser (6'2", 225) So.*
	23	John Cousins (6'2", 220) Sr.*

MLB	45	Mike Pollard (6'0", 225) Jr.*
	36	Aaron Graham (6'1", 235) Jr.

* = used redshirt season

Depth Charts

WLB	1	Frank Strong (6'1", 220) Sr.
	45	Mike Pollard (6'0", 225) Jr.*
CB	42	Kris Richard (5'11", 190) Sr.*
	30	Kevin Arbet (5'11", 180) Jr.
SS	43	Troy Polamalu (5'10", 210) Jr.
	27	Jason Leach (5'11", 200) Fr.*
FS	5	DeShaun Hill (5'11", 200) Jr.*
	6	Antuan Simmons (5'10", 195) Sr.*
CB	6	Antuan Simmons (5'10", 195) Sr.*
	29	Chris Cash (5'11", 170) Sr.

Special Teams

P	38	Mike MacGillivray (5'10", 195) Sr.*
PK	48	David Davis (5'11", 160) Jr.*
	15	David Newbury (5'9", 175) Sr.
SNP	50	Matt Hayward (6'2", 225) So.
	64	Joe Boskovich (6'4", 225) So.*
HLD	38	Mike MacGillivray (5'10", 195) Sr.*
	10	Matt Cassel (6'5", 220) Fr.*
KOR	83	Keary Colbert (6'1", 195) So.
	82	D. Hale (6'1", 185) So.*
	22	Darrell Rideaux (5'9", 170) Jr.

* = used redshirt season

PR	30	Kevin Arbet (5'11", 180) Jr.
	2	Kareem Kelly (6'0", 190) Jr.

2002 DEPTH CHART
Offense

SE	2	Kareem Kelly (6'0", 190) Sr.
	1	Mike Williams (6'5", 210) Fr.

LT	77	Jacob Rogers (6'6", 305) Jr.*
	66	Eric Torres (6'5", 300) Jr.*

LG	78	Lenny Vandermade (6'3", 275) Jr.*
	66	Eric Torres (6'5", 300) Jr.*

C	62	Norm Katnik (6'4", 280) Jr.*
	73	Derek Graf (6'4", 280) Sr.*

RG	69	Zach Wilson (6'5", 300) Sr.*
	66	Eric Torres (6'5", 300) Jr.*

RT	74	Winston Justice (6'6", 305) Fr.
	66	Eric Torres (6'5", 300) Jr.*

TE	81	Alex Holmes (6'3", 265) Jr.
	44	Gregg Guenther Jr. (6'8", 245) So.*

QB	3	Carson Palmer (6'6", 230) Sr.*
	10	Matt Cassel (6'5", 225) So.*
	11	Matt Leinart (6'5", 215) Fr.*

* = used redshirt season

| FB | 21 | Malaefou MacKenzie (5'11", 225) Sr.* |
| | 34 | Chad Pierson (6'1", 240) Sr.* |

TB	25	Justin Fargas (6'1", 210) Sr.*
	4	Sultan McCullough (6'0", 190) Sr.*
	26	Hershel Dennis (5'11", 175) Fr.

| FL | 83 | Keary Colbert (6'1", 205) Jr. |
| | 87 | Grant Mattos (6'3", 225) Sr. |

Defense

| DE | 94 | Kenechi Udeze (6'4", 280) So.* |
| | 91 | Van Brown (6'5", 255) So.* |

| NT | 99 | Mike Patterson (6'0", 285) So. |
| | 93 | Bernard Riley (6'3", 320) Sr. |

| DT | 84 | Shaun Cody (6'4", 275) So |
| | 93 | Bernard Riley (6'3", 320) Sr. |

| DE | 56 | Omar Nazel (6'5", 240) Jr.* |
| | 88 | Doyal Butler (6'3", 245) Sr. |

| SLB | 6 | Matt Grootegoed (5'11", 205) So.* |
| | 42 | Dallas Sartz (6'5", 210) Fr. |

| MLB | 45 | Mike Pollard (6'0", 225) Sr.* |
| | 51 | Melvin Simmons (6'1", 215) Jr.* |

| WLB | 51 | Melvin Simmons (6'1", 215) Jr.* |
| | 41 | Bobby Otani (6'0", 210) So. |

* = used redshirt season

CB	8	Marcell Allmond (6'0", 200) Jr.*
	31	William Buchanon (6'4", 175) Fr.*
SS	43	Troy Polamalu (5'10", 215) Sr.
	27	Jason Leach (5'11", 210) So.*
FS	5	DeShaun Hill (5'11", 200) Sr.*
	27	Jason Leach (5'11", 210) So.*
CB	22	Darrell Rideaux (5'8", 170) Sr.
	24	Justin Wyatt (5'10", 175) Fr.

Special Teams

P	14	Tom Malone (6'0", 185) Fr.
PK	16	Ryan Killeen (5'11", 210) So.
	48	David Davis (5'11", 160, Sr.*
SNP	50	Matt Hayward (6'1", 215) Jr.
	64	Joe Boskovich (6'4", 240) Jr.*
HLD	14	Tom Malone (6'0", 185) Fr.
KOR	8	Marcell Allmond (6'0", 200) Jr.*
	25	Justin Fargas (6'1", 210) Sr.*
	26	Hershel Dennis (5'11", 175) Fr.
PR	19	Greig Carlson (5'10", 185) Fr.*
	2	Kareem Kelly (6'0", 190) Sr.

* = used redshirt season

2003 DEPTH CHART
Offense

SE	1	Mike Williams (6'5", 230) So.
	15	Jason Mitchell (6'1", 200) Jr.*
LT	77	Jacob Rogers (6'6", 305) Sr.*
	76	Nate Steinbacher (6'5", 305) Sr.*
LG	78	Lenny Vandermade (6'3", 275) Sr.*
	63	Travis Watkins (6'3", 305) Jr.*
C	62	Norm Katnik (6'4", 280) Sr.*
	67	Ryan Kalil (6'4", 270) Fr.
RG	57	Fred Matua (6'2", 300) Fr.*
	66	Eric Torres (6'5", 300) Sr.*
RT	74	Winston Justice (6'6", 300) So.
	75	Kyle Williams (6'6", 290) Fr.*
TE	44	Gregg Guenther Jr. (6'8", 245) Jr.*
	86	Dominique Byrd (6'3", 255) So.
QB	11	Matt Leinart (6'5", 220) So.*
	10	Matt Cassel (6'5", 220) Jr.*
	17	John David Booty (6'3", 200) Fr.
	8	Brandon Hance (6'1", 195) Jr.*
FB	40	Brandon Hancock (6'1", 235) So.
	35	Lee Webb (6'0", 240) Jr.*
	37	David Kirtman (6'0", 220) So.*

* = used redshirt season

TB	34	Hershel Dennis (5'11", 190) So.
	21	LenDale White (6'2", 225) Fr.
	5	Reggie Bush (6'0", 190) Fr.

| FL | 83 | Keary Colbert (6'2", 210) Sr. |
| | 2 | Steve Smith (6'1", 190) Fr. |

Defense

| DE | 94 | Kenechi Udeze (6'4", 285) Jr.* |
| | 91 | Van Brown (6'5", 265) Jr.* |

| NT | 99 | Mike Patterson (6'0", 285) Jr. |
| | 52 | LaJuan Ramsey (6'3", 270) So. |

| DT | 84 | Shaun Cody (6'4", 285) Jr. |
| | 91 | Manuel Wright (6'6", 285) Fr. |

| DE | 56 | Omar Nazel (6'5", 245) Sr.* |
| | 90 | Frostee Rucker (6'4", 240) So.* |

| SLB | 6 | Matt Grootegoed (5'11", 215) Jr.* |
| | 42 | Dallas Sartz (6'5", 220) So. |

| MLB | 58 | Lofa Tatupu (6'0", 225) So.* |
| | 51 | Melvin Simmons (6'1", 220) Sr.* |

| WLB | 51 | Melvin Simmons (6'1", 220) Sr.* |
| | 59 | Collin Ashton (6'1", 215) So.* |

* = used redshirt season

CB	28	Will Poole (6'0", 190) Sr.*
	23	Ronald Nunn (5'11", 180) Jr.*
	24	Justin Wyatt (5'10", 180) So.
SS	20	Darnell Bing (6'2", 220) Fr.
	43	Mike Ross (6'0", 175) So.
FS	27	Jason Leach (5'11", 210) Jr.*
	26	Greg Farr (6'0", 195, Sr.)
CB	8	Marcell Allmond (6'0", 200) Sr.*
	23	Ronald Nunn (5'11", 180) Jr.*
	24	Justin Wyatt (5'10", 180) So.

Special Teams

P	14	Tom Malone (6'0", 190) So.
PK	16	Ryan Killeen (5'11", 200) Jr.
SNP	50	Matt Hayward (6'1", 225) Sr.
	64	Joe Boskovich (6'4", 240) Sr.*
HLD	14	Tom Malone (6'0", 190) So.
KOR	5	Reggie Bush (6'0", 190, Fr.)
	8	Marcell Allmond (6'0", 200) Sr.*
PR	19	Greig Carlson (5'10", 195) So.*
	5	Reggie Bush (6'0", 190) Fr.

* = used redshirt season

2004 DEPTH CHART
Offense

SE	8	Dwayne Jarrett (6'5", 195) Fr.
	82	Chris McFoy (6'1", 195) So.*
LT	79	Sam Baker (6'5", 290) Fr.
	75	Kyle Williams (6'6", 290) So.*
LG	73	John Drake (6'4", 350) Sr.
	53	Jeff Byers (6'3", 275) Fr.
	63	Travis Watkins (6'3", 305) Sr.*
C	67	Ryan Kalil (6'4", 270) So.
	53	Jeff Byers (6'3", 275) Fr.
RG	51	Fred Matua (6'2", 305) So.*
	60	Drew Radovich (6'5", 290) Fr.*
RT	71	Taitusi Lutui (6'6", 370) Jr.
	75	Kyle Williams (6'6", 290) So.*
TE	81	Alex Holmes (6'3", 270) Sr.*
	86	Dominique Byrd (6'3", 260) Jr.
QB	11	Matt Leinart (6'5", 225) Jr.*
	10	Matt Cassel (6'5", 230) Sr.*
	4	Brandon Hance (6'1", 195) Sr.*
FB	35	Lee Webb (6'0", 240) Sr.*
	37	David Kirtman (6'0", 225) Jr.*

* = used redshirt season

TB	21	LenDale White (6'2", 235) So.
	5	Reggie Bush (6'0", 200) So.
	22	Desmond Reed (5'9", 180) Fr.*

FL	2	Steve Smith (6'1", 195) So.
	15	Jason Mitchell (6'1", 200) Sr.*

Defense

DE	90	Frostee Rucker (6'4", 255) Jr.*
	54	Jeff Schweiger (6'4", 250) Fr.

NT	99	Mike Patterson (6'0", 290) Sr.
	49	Sedrick Ellis (6'2", 275) Fr.*

DT	84	Shaun Cody (6'4", 295) Sr.
	92	Manuel Wright (6'6", 290) So.
	52	LaJuan Ramsey (6'3", 285) Jr.

DE	96	Lawrence Jackson (6'5", 250) Fr.*
	84	Shaun Cody (6'4", 295) Sr.

SLB	42	Dallas Sartz (6'5", 220) Jr.
	41	Thomas Williams (6'3", 225) Fr.*

MLB	58	Lofa Tatupu (6'0", 225) Jr.*
	59	Collin Ashton (6'1", 215) Jr.*

WLB	6	Matt Grootegoed (5'11", 215) Sr.*
	55	Keith Rivers (6'3", 220, Fr.)

* = used redshirt season

CB	24	Justin Wyatt (5'10", 180) Jr.
	25	Eric Wright (5'11", 190) Fr.*
	28	Terrell Thomas (6'2", 195) Fr.*
SS	20	Darnell Bing (6'2", 220) So.
	27	Jason Leach (5'11", 210) Sr.*
FS	27	Jason Leach (5'11", 210) Sr.*
	29	Scott Ware (6'3", 220) Jr.
CB	25	Eric Wright (5'11", 190) Fr.*
	30	Kevin Arbet (5'11", 190) Sr.*
	23	Ronald Nunn (5'11", 180) Sr.*

Special Teams

P	14	Tom Malone (6'0", 190) Jr.
PK	16	Ryan Killeen (5'11", 185) Sr.
	19	Mario Danelo (5'10", 210) Fr.*
SNP	59	Collin Ashton (6'1", 215) Jr.*
	50	Will Collins (6'2", 220) Fr.*
HLD	14	Tom Malone (6'0", 190) Jr.
KOR	5	Reggie Bush (6'0", 200) So.
	22	Desmond Reed (5'9", 180) Fr.*
PR	5	Reggie Bush (6'0", 200) So.
	19	Greig Carlson (5'10", 195) Jr.*

Index

Index

Index

Index

Index